The Sat▨▨▨▨

A Catholic Viewpoint on Television

Dedication

This book is dedicated to my father, Kennett David Bawden, who first named the television the Satan Box in the late 1960's. He noticed how it dominated and neutralized resistance to the corruption going on in the world at that time. May he rest in peace.

Cover art

At Quito, Ecuador the Blessed Virgin warned: "The third meaning of the (sanctuary) lamp's going out is that those times the air will be filled with the spirit of impurity which like a deluge of filth will flood the streets, squares and public places. The licentiousness will be such there will be no more virgin souls in the world." Today the air is literally filled with impurity beaming down on us from 20,000 miles above us from satellites. Look at the menu on a satellite receiver and this is easily verified. Not only is pornography relatively available, but many other programs that are unsuitable for anyone. Meditate on what a virgin soul is. And how many souls lose their virginity the moment they reach the age of reason?

Table of Contents

Introduction

Since its wide spread introduction into the world in the 1950's television has become the most influential invention of all time. There is no question that television has radically changed the way the world operates and the way people think. In the United States 99 percent of homes have televisions. Actually it is probably higher as few homes don't have a television. It is not socially correct not to have a television or to advocate getting rid of the television, although there is a small vocal minority advocating just that.

Our homes have been redesigned to accommodate television. How many have a TV room instead of a family room. Some even have a true home theater and the television has been called a home theater. And how many televisions do people have? Not only is there a TV room but there is often a television in the bedrooms.

And then go out into the world today. How many public places have a television running. In fact, it is some times hard to get away from the television, when out in public.

Television has changed our lives.

There have been several secular books written on television and the media and several websites devoted to a critical look at both. Although we will consult these sources for some of our information, the main focus of this work is a Catholic viewpoint on television.

The Church has not said a great deal officially about television, because it is such a new invention. However, the Church has said a great deal over the centuries about the components of television, such as the theater. Since the television is a *home theater*, the timeless teaching of the Fathers of the Church and the saints can be applied easily to television. As radio and movies came in, there are some decrees and statements from the Popes on these technologies, which can be applied also to television.

It is time for a critical look at the most influential invention in world history. It is time for a thoroughly Catholic view of television. This book is offered as this.

Saint Ambrose writes: "I am of the opinion that one should not only avoid frequent plays, but all plays." [1] If we apply this to television, then we should avoid habitual viewing certainly and consider giving up

---

[1] Dignity and Duties of the Priest, Saint Alphonsus, page 351.

television entirely. This may be a hard saying, but it is something that must be considered most seriously in the light of the facts. True Pope Pius XII gives reserved praise for television in an Encyclical on the subject, but this praise is reserved and new evidence has come to light that was not available before Pope Pius XII died. Some may decide right now to give up television. Others may decide to investigate the matter more deeply. The exercises in the next chapter are essential for anyone who has not yet decided to give up television entirely. In fact, your eternal salvation depends on making these exercises and finishing studying this important book.

Some of the information in this book repeats, but how many people are happy to watch rerun after rerun on television?

Watching Yourself Watch Television

Let us consider a few questions. How must television do I actually watch? What do I watch? Is it good for me or is it bad for me? In order to apply the principles in this book to make our lives better we must first find out where we are at spiritually and materially in regard to the television. And so let us follow a three week program.

Week 1

In the first week keep track of what you do in a typical day without changing your habits. Note when you watch television and what you are watching. At the end of the week, add up how many hours of television you have watched.

Week 2

In the second week, we get a bit more critical. In addition to noting what and when you watch, rate each program. Did it do what you wanted, when you watched it. For instance, did you learn anything from the documentary? Was the recreational program truly entertaining? And above all, starting asking the question, was the program moral or immoral?

Week 3

In the third week and throughout the rest of the program, reduce your television viewing to an hour per day. Choose programs carefully and rate them, when you are finished. Want to watch a two hour movie, then take a day off from television. Yes, you can live without television for a day. In fact, there are people who have gone to the fourth week of the program that inspired this one, that is giving up television entirely. A man in the late 1990's took his television outside and shot it with a shotgun. He says it is the best thing he ever did. We may not be required to go this far, but in examining the information gathered in these three weeks we will soon realize just how much more careful we need to be with the satan box.

No TV Week

There is a website devoted to this movement to have a No TV Week each year. Let us consider their definition of No TV Week:

No T.V. Week is a week in which Acts of Love is asking families across the world to turn off the television and pick up a book while also spending essential time together as a family.

One week without television is an opportunity for young people to grow their imagination while developing better character.

According to the A.C. Nielsen Co., the average American watches more than 4 hours of TV each day (or 28 hours/week, or 2 months of nonstop TV-watching per year). In a 65-year life, that person will have spent 9 years glued to the tube.

In our study we will find that television is incompatible with the penitential seasons of the year, according to the Fathers of the Church and even Church Councils. Holy Week should always be a no TV week.

Taking a week away from the television, we will find that television is consuming a great deal of our time. What are we going to do with all of this time that we have suddenly freed up?

Try talking to God and letting God talk to you rather than spending time watching and listening to the satan box.

Indiscriminate use of the radio and television by young or old is a pathetic disregard for good morals and artistic taste. Not only parents and guardians, but the entire family should be concerned over the programs that are watched and heard. Late evening programs are generally directed to the interest of adults.

Children are too immature to watch such programs. It is the duty of parents that children are in bed where they should be when these programs are presented. We should consult the evaluation of television, radio and theatre offerings which our better critics make available to us in the Catholic Press.

Television and Children

The Legion of Decency, before its demise in the 1960's, rated films in three basic categories, A, B and C. A was acceptable for all, B only for adults and C was condemned and unacceptable for anyone. This type of system is fine for a movie theater, but not for television. If a program cannot be rated as A, acceptable for all, it cannot be viewed in a home where children live.

Consider the picture above. While the mother is hustling the children off to bed, their father is watching something that is unacceptable for children on the television. When these children get a chance, their curiosity will lead them to watch these programs at someone else's house or some other place. This picture is from the late 1950's, when there was only one television in the house. Today, when the children may have access to a television of their own, what is to prevent them from switching over to see what daddy is watching?

And this picture is from the time, when there was a *family hour* on television, considered suitable for the viewing of all, keeping the more mature themes for the later evening.

We cannot be too cautious in these days of utter apostasy and amorality in the protection of the innocent. The television is the greatest pervayer of filth and ruiner of souls today! Unfortunately many parents are tempted to use the television as a babysitter for their children, exposing them to this danger without taking the necessary precautions. Many parents will prudently lock the television away in a closet or sell it rather than take a chance that their children will be perverted.

In 1947 at the beatification of Blessed Maria Goretti, Pope Pius XII stated, There rises to Our lips the cry of the Saviour: "Woe to the world because of scandals!" (Matthew 18:7). Woe to those who consciously and deliberately spread corruption-in novels, newspapers, magazines, theaters, films, (on television), in a world of immodesty! Woe to the degraded youth who with refined and delicate incision strikes deadly infection deep into a virgin heart! Woe to those fathers and mothers who for want of energy and prudence yield to the caprices of their sons and daughters, renounce their paternal and maternal authority, which in them is a reflection of the divine authority! But woe, too, to all those deluded Christians in name only, who could rise to the situation and who would find themselves backed by legions of good upright people ready to combat scandal with every means at their disposal, but do not!

Strong words, "Woe to those fathers and mothers who for want of energy and prudence yield to the caprices of their sons and daughters, renounce their paternal and maternal authority." God gave you this authority to bring people to heaven, not to assist them in their own damnation! Such parents, who watch all manner of evil on the

Satan box and allow their children the same license, shall burn very hot in hell!

In his Encyclical Casti Conubii, Pope Pius XI reminds us, "For now, alas, not secretly nor under cover, but openly, with all sense of shame put aside, now by word, again by writings, by theatrical productions of every kind, by motion pictures portraying vivid scenes, addresses broadcast by means of radio, in short by all the inventions of modern science, the sanctity of marriage is trampled upon and derided. Divorce, adultery, all the basest vices, either are extolled or at least are depicted in such colors as to appear free of all reproach and infamy.

"These thoughts are instilled into men of every class, rich and poor, workers and masters, lettered and unlettered, married and single, godly and godless, old and young: but for these last, an easier prey, the worst snares are laid."

Indeed the worst snares are laid for innocent children, who can learn all manner of evil even before they have reached the age of reason. Can one be surprised that when they are exposed to such rampant evil that they fast become skillful mortal sinners? We must teach children how to seek what is good and avoid what is evil, but how can we do so if we ourselves are dead and seek pleasure and vice, rather than prayer and penance?

Pope Pius XII commenting on the Apostolate of Enviroment, Address to Italian Catholic Action on September 20, 1942 states, "One can't even imagine the depth of moral corruption to which some authors, editors, artists and others who spread such literary, dramatic, artistic and pictorial works, have not feared to descend. They have changed the use of pen, art, industrial progress and wonderful modern inventions into means and producers of immorality. One sees the adolescent with the fires of passion awakening, plunged into this type of nourishment for his spirit and his eyes. One sees parents taking their sons and daughters to these spectacles. Thus, in their youthful hearts, instead of innocent and holy images, there are impressed deadly desires and pictures which often will never be erased. "

"Thus, in their youthful hearts, instead of innocent and holy images, there are impressed deadly desires and pictures which often will never be erased." When Pope Pius XII wrote this the television was still in the developmental stages and these dangers were at least down the street. And yet in a few years he would warn:

In a letter to Bishops of Italy, January 1, 1954, Pope Pius XII says, "We have constantly before Our mind the painful spectacle of the power for evil and moral ruin of cinema films. How, then, can We not be horrified at the thought that this poisoned atmosphere of materialism, or frivolity, of hedonism, which too often is found in so many theaters, can by means of television be brought into the very sanctuary of the home? Really, one cannot imagine anything more fatal to the spiritual health of a country than to rehearse before so many innocent souls, even within the family circle, those lurid scenes of forbidden pleasure, passion and evil which can undermine and bring to lasting ruin a formation of purity, goodness and healthy personal and social upbringing."

Pope Pius XII compares the home to a sanctuary. Indeed the home, which is formed by the Sacrament of Marriage, should be a sanctuary where the parents and children can seek after salvation away from the dangers of the world. And yet these very dangers can be brought in by turning one switch. All the filth of the districts of the city, which a person would never enter can be brought into his own living room! Beware of these dangers. Home should be a place of tranquility and true peace, where the various family members can find quiet away from the cares of the world.

On January 4, 1954 addressing the Italian Teachers Union, Pope Pius XII stated, "The young man whose holidays are sanctified by his having met whatever task or difficulty that lay in his path, who goes often to Holy Communion (Or in these times, makes spiritual Communions often), who is truthful and loyal, who is quick to help the needy, who respects girlhood and womanhood, and has the strength to shut his eyes and his heart to all that is impure in books, pictures and films-that young man shows that he does truly possess a living faith. And note well that if faith is not living, neither is it active. If others often invest so much energy and effort in the enterprises of the evil one, how much greater will have to be your zeal for the cause of God, of Christ, of the Church!"

Children must be taught to turn away from evil. They are taught, not by our numerous words, but by our actions. We can preach against evil morning, noon and night, but if we indulge in it once a day for even a thirty minute television program, they shall follow our bad example, rather than our constant preaching. And yet many indulge in evil morning, noon and night and fail to speak against it even once. Remember that in times of great evil, we must counter with great faith, faith so as to remove mountains, and this faith is worthless, if we do not remove the mountains of evil around us, as far as we are able, by turning off the radio and television and avoiding all other forms of evil surrounding us today.

In his 1948 address to parish priests and lenten preachers, Pope Pius XII reminds us, "Yet the doctrine of truth is no less attractive, and heroism of virtue no less stimulating, provided that they are not given forth with the coldness of theorem or the dryness of an article of law.

"If the movies play primarily upon the imagination, the doctrine of faith is an effective antidote. It exacts from the young person mental penetration and application. It demands that he learn to judge and distinguish the true from the false, the good from the evil, the licit from the illicit. Do not flee or avoid any difficulty: your young people must have assurance that you can tell them everything that they can ask you, and confide in you."

Pope Pius XII prescribes the cure for the evil today, the doctrine of faith. We must teach children how to judge, how to tell good from evil, true from false and what is permitted from what is forbidden.

We must consider that television is just one form of materialism, which must be decried today. Materialism has led us to seek a soft life free from any true effort, and in 1953 Pope Pius XII warned us about technological materialism, which is now infecting the world. How many have gone into debt to purchase modern technology, when they have no need for the device? Is a radio or television a necessity? Absolutely not! And to become a slave of another through usurious debt for a luxury is a sin, especially if it leads to other sins.

> Pope Pius XII on Christmas Eve 1953 warned us, "We cannot, however, omit calling attention to the new forms of materialism which the technological spirit introduces into life. Whereever technology reigns supreme, there human society will be transformed into a colorless mass, into something impersonal and without substance, and this contrary to the clear designs of nature and the Creator. And with particular anxiety We consider the danger threatening the family, which is the strongest principle of order in the society. For the family is capable of inspiring in its members innumerable daily acts of service; it binds them to the home and hearth with the bonds of affection and awakens in each of them a love of the family traditions in the production and conservation of useful good."

Many advances today can be used to give us more time to discharge our more important duties, such as the education of children. One may even be permitted to go into debt to purchase these items, but in these cases prudent advice should always be sought. We have many devices, which reduce the amount of time needed to take care of our material chores, such as the microwave, the washer and dryer, etc. The extra time is called for to teach children at home and to pursue spiritual studies for ourself and to teach others.

Dangers for Boys and Girls

In <u>Helps to Purity</u>, pages 187 and 188 we read: "Selling flowers or papers on the street at night. Delaying to answer the calls of nature; e.g., during school Carrying messages, papers or telegrams to dens of vice. Companions. The good may become bad. Housekeepers who lay in a barrel of apples won't content themselves with an occasional look at the top of the barrel to remove the rotten ones. Parents must question children day by day about their chum's actions and conversations; nor let boys and girls play out of their sight in alleys, basements, barns, or in lonesome and dark places. How guilty are those parents who, under the plea of distracting or amusing their children, take them once or twice a week to theatres or shows, where they are exposed to the two-fold fever of music and of scenic representations. The same blame attaches to the toleration of sensual literature.

"As good books help in making saints, bad ones largely share in producing devils incarnate."

"But scenic representation more vividly affects the mind and leave a more lasting impression than mere reading does. Hence as all kinds of CRIMES ARE PROTRAYED AND CONDONED in many moving-picture shows, are these not the very factory of criminals? Therefore city authorities should everywhere exercise a rigorous censorship and mercilessly exclude all objectionable films.

"Light is the normal excitant of the retina, but a profusion os light hurts that marvelous membrane, so that it becomes incapable of perceiving it, whereby it may forever lose its power of perception. Repeated shocks which spontaneous and provoked emotions impress upon the brains may likewise harmfully affect the integrity of reason and health." - <u>Popular Discourses on Hygiene, Amusements, Theatrical Play, Music, etc</u>, by J.B. Fonssagrives, M.D.

Pledge of the Legion of Decency

In the name of the Father and of the Son and of the Holy Ghost. Amen.

I condemn indecent and immoral motion pictures, and those which glorify crime or criminals.

I promise to do what I can do to strengthen public opinion against the production of indecent and immoral films, and to unite with all who protest against them.

I acknowledge my obligation to form a right conscience about pictures that are dangerous to moral life. As a member of the Legion of Decency, I pledge myself to remain away from them. I promise, further, to stay away altogether from places of amusement which show them as a matter of policy.

Unfortunately the Legion of Decency no longer exists and never addressed television. The Legion of decency went out of business about the same time Paul VI eliminated the Index of Prohibited Books and Canon 1399 from the Code of Canon Law. The shepherds no longer safe guarded the sheep.

Television Hypnotizes

What few realize is that their ideas of right and wrong are manipulated by television to obtain the ends of advertisers, etc. This manipulation is done to sell products, products we don't often need and sometimes do not even want. These products are often harmful to us, and therefore we must avoid them under the Natural Law.

In a book <u>The Hidden Persuaders</u>, Vance Packard states (page 1): "This book is an attempt to explore a strange and rather exotic new area of American life. It is about the large-scale efforts being made, often with impressive success, to channel our unthinking habits, our purchasing decisions, and our thought processes by the use of the insights gleaned from psychiatry and the social sciences. Typically these efforts take place beneath our level of awareness; so that the appeals which move us are often, in a sense, "hidden". The result is that many of us are being influenced and manipulted, far more than we realize, in the patterns of our every day lives."

In the chapter entitled The Built-in Sexual Overtone, Mr. Packard begins (page 79): "Infatuation with one's own body is an infantile trait that ... persists in many an adult's subconscious ... The ethics of exploiting it ... to sell goods ... are something else.

"The potency of sex as a sales promoter was not, of course, an original discovery of the depth merchandisers. Sex images have long been cherished by ad men purely as eye stoppers with the depth approach, sex began taking on some interesting twists, ramifications, and subtleties."

Many advertisements on television today are per se (i.e. of themselves) immoral, as We shall consider later on.

On page 166 Mr. Packard states, that it is going further: "The aim now is nothing less than to influence the state of our mind and to channel our behaviour..."

Indeed through the media our behaviour has been channeled in some frightening ways.

How many today are mesmerized by the System of Antichrist just as the snake mesmerizes the bird in order to devour him. There is an inordinate curiosity that will kill just as certainly as the snake will devour the bird he has hypnotized. We spend entirely too much time devoted to a study of the System of Antichrist, which should be devoted to a study of the System of Christ the King which we are supposed to implement in our lives and in the world. How can we bring about the reign of Christ the King, if we do not know His Law for us?

In his book The People Shapers, Vance Packard states (page 164): "The hypnotist does not need to be in the same room with the subject in order to put him into a trance. He can in fact be miles away. One way to hypnotize by remote control is television.

"The hypnotist Herbert Spiegel demonstrated this in an experiment at Columbia. A subject known to be hypnotizable sat in a lounge chair before a TV set. Spiegel was seated before a closed-circuit TV camera four stories below. He talked to the subject just as if the subject were in the same room and put him into a trance. On another case it was a thirty-year old male stranger. While the man was in a trance Spiegel told him that his hands were locked together, and the subject found this to be true. Then Spiegel told the man that he, the subject, was not going out of the trance but that his hands would remain locked until Spiegel came up to him and tapped him on the head. After waiting a while for an elevator, Spiegel entered the room and found the subject normally composed except his hands were locked firmly together. Spiegel tapped his head and his hands parted.

"Spiegel suggests that televised hypnosis could have a number of uses. It could be used in group therapy and mass education. (There is some evidence that simple rote learning can be enhanced by the mental relaxation that goes with hypnosis.) But Spiegel warns that the technique could have dangerous consequences if used in any way in public broadcasts. He has called for stringent controls as a safety measure."

We can be assured that the safety measures have not been enacted and this experiment reported in 1965 has been perfected.

Wes Moore wrote an article <u>Television: Opiate of the Masses</u>. [2] In this he states: "Paraphysiologist Thomas Mulholland found that after just 30 seconds of watching telvision the brain begins to produce alpha waves, which indicates torpid (almost comatose) rates of activity. Alpha brain waves are associated with unfocused, overly receptive states of consciousness. A high frequency alpha waves does not occur normally when the eyes are open. In fact, Mulholland's research implies that watching television is neurologically analogous to staring at a blank wall.

"I should note that the goal of hypnosis is to induce slow brain wave states. Alpha waves are present during the "light hypnotic" state used by hypnotherapists for suggestion therapy."

The greatest mesmerizer and tool of Satan is the television. On this altar is sacrificed much time, which should have been devoted to far better uses. Through this medium the System of Antichrist has destroyed several generations, and led them into the most perverse of errors and vices. If they do not participate directly in vice, they participate indirectly through the means of television. The television which has such a great potential for good has been used for great evil, evil which would otherwise be impossible.

The question We are here considering is whether television can be used for even more perverse ends through hypnosis. The term mesmerized, which We have used comes from the conspirator Mesmer, who is the first modern person to use hypnosis through his heretical magnetic theory which even modern science rejects. This magnetic theory however has been adopted by the Masons and other conspirators, who praise Mesmer. Due to the lack of accurate scientific

---

[2]   http://www.cognitiveliberty.org/5jcl/5JCL59.htm Form <u>The Journal of Cognivitie Liberties</u>, volume 2, issue 2, pages 59-66, 2001 copyright

information and the laxity of Our Predecessors, a definitive statement on hypnotism is impossible. However, We can reach a probable opinion based on the information at hand and Our own observations.

Hypnosis is a nervous sleep induced by artificial external means. As such it is not true restful sleep, but rather a sleep-like state. Although those watching television may appear half asleep, they are not truly resting and therefore after watching will not be restored, as sleep would have restored them, unless they truly fell asleep. Although television may be a recreation, just as the actual attendance at the event depicted would be a recreation or change of scenery, which restores, overuse is not advisable.

Braid, an early hypnotist who perfected and corrected the theories of Mesmer, stated, "fatigue the eyes in order to fatigue the brain." With television one need not perform any action, but merely sit still and be fatigued. In fact there are people who will become fixated on television to the point that they appear in a hypnotic or semi-hypnotic state. To illustrate this the following experiment may be performed:

Hypnosis can be brought about by fixing the eyes on a single object or a bright object. The television is just such an object. Since the eyes need not move while watching television, they become fixed and one stares at the television. Hypnosis can be brought about by tiring the eyes through staring. To prove that people are in a state resembling hypnosis, We ask you to perform the following experiment:

In a room with several people of varying Intelligence Quotients (IQ's) with a moral television program going, have a look about the room after the program has been running awhile and you will probably see several symptoms of hynotism. You will see people with glazed over eyes and a total lack of movement. We have performed this experiment and the sight was shocking.

"Basically hypnosis is brought on by one or more of the following things:

"1. fixity of look, which is had because the television is fixed in one place and one need not look about, as one would at a movie, sporting event or play.

"2. this fixity is on a brilliant object, and the television is brilliant.

"3. watching the television, one's eyes are converged on one point, which can also hypnotize.

"4. The television is a sustained and monotonous sensation, which also can bring about hypnosis.

"5. The television lastly is also a vivid sensory impression."

Although the subject must consent to hypnosis, once a person has consented to a hypnotist, that hypnotist can rehypnotize them at will. Whether the television can hypnotize everyone or only a few, science must determine, and We reserve final judgement on this point until science can provide more information. However, We know that there is a minority who certainly can be hypnotized by television, and for these, just as for the alcoholic who cannot drink one ounce of liquor without continuing on to drunkenness, these people must abstain completely. For some temperance or moderation means total abstinence, because they cannot partake moderately.

One will notice several symptoms of the second stage of hypnosis, lethargy, in those who watch an inordinant amount of television. The symptoms of lethargy are a great lack of energy, inertness, total indifference, apathy, dullness and slugishness. These symptoms sound like the description of the couch potato, who sits morning, noon and night, or every possible moment in front of the television.

Rev. Alexander E. Sanford M.D. in his work Pastoral Medicine, on pages 159 and 160 notes the following: "The state of hypnotism consists in an expressly provoked loosening, even in partly unfastening, the normally fast ties between physical and corporeal events. But if loosened once, or even frequently, this tie undoubtedly loses its enduring security, ... Exactly the same symptoms, as expressly provoked in hypnotising, are known to the physicians as primary symptoms of hysteria. ... Hypnosis is nothing else but an artificially provoked hysteria."

Note well, that an important tie between physical and corporeal events is loosened in hypnosis. Therefore as with all serious operations, a proportionately serious reason must be had to permit one to operate. One may not operate to remove a healthy organ, therefore one may not hypnotise without a serious cause, and even in this case hypnosis may be found to be forbidden, although We do not currently possess sufficient information to render a final decision. Certainly one could not be hypnotised by anyone but a learned Catholic, who is well versed in moral theology and obeys the natural law.

The symptoms of hysteria, can be found in the television addict, which may indicate a further connection between television and hypnosis:

1. A morbid state of autosuggestion. (i.e. self-induced suggestibility)

2. An exagerated form of egotism. Just try and tell the television-addict, that he must unplug his drug. He may bear with many things, but not this, his addiction being removed.

3. Excessive fickleness of the emotions

4. Lack of truth. (i.s. systematic lying, born of a deluded imagination.) Everyone, who is self-centered will lie about their pet vice. The alcoholic, who says I can quit any time I want to, comes to mind.

5. Sins against the virtue of temperance, such as lust, drunkenenss or gluttony.

Fr. Sanford gives a simple cure for hysteria, perfect obedience to a spiritual director (i.e. a spiritual director authorized by the Church), performing works of charity and ceasing to think much about themselves.

Hypnotism can produce injury to health and/or weakened memory, reason or will power. Indeed television can produce all of these evils, the only question to be answered whether these evils result from hypnotism or some other cause.

There is another danger of television, which has not been before considered, and that is the problem of brain washing. We know that the conspiracy has used overt forms of brain washing on people, as has been reported about prisoners of war taken in conflicts after World War II, such as Korea and Vietnam. In Korea there were no escapes. Many consider that the first duty of a prisoner of war is to escape, in fact during World War II, unless the situation was hopeless, we see many examples of excape and attempted escape. It is logical to assume and simple observation affirms that covert forms of brain washing are being used on the masses in so-called free countries. If one can watch some of the advertising on television without becoming angry at the obvious violation of natural law suggested, one must be aware that one has accepted such violations. Several commercials from a large corporation come to mind. They use simple slogans, which are contrary to virtue and the natural law, such as Gotta have it; Sometimes you gotta break the rules; Have it your way; The choice of a new generation, as if there is any difference between generations.

Those, who are truly seeking salvation, see only accidental differences between generations, such as the biological effects of age, etc. In their heart, they see no difference between the teenager seeking sanctity and the octagenarian seeking sanctity. The teenager and the octagenerian, who are both seeking sanctity have more in common, than they do with those seeking sins of their own age group. There can be truly no generation gap, except in the most superficial and meaningless things. It is interesting that this corporation (Pepsico) has shown its true colors in distributing bumper stickers telling people that if they must drink and drive they should drink their non-alcoholic drink, while at the same time striking a deal to trade their soft-drink with Russia for one of the most dangerous of alcoholic drinks, vodka.

Four Reasons for the Elimination of Television

We shall now consider some of the arguments from Jerry Mander in his book, <u>Four Reasons for the Elimination of Television</u>, written in 1978. We will remember that this man is a member of the Sierra club and probably a member of the New Age or similar antichristian movement. However, as we know from St. Thomas, even the pagans can have truthful ideas. (St. Thomas quotes often from the Philosopher, Aristotle, and other pagans, praising their truth and correcting their error.)

On page 194 he reports: "For the entire four hours or more per day that the average person is watching television, the repetitive process of constructing images out of dots, following scans, and vibrating with the beats of the set and the exigencies of electronic rhythm goes on. It was this repetitive, nonstop requirement to reconstruct images that are conciously usable that caused McLuhan to call television "participatory", another unfortunate choice of words. It suggest exactly the opposite of what is going on.

"I wish he had said "overpowering." ... In fact, watching television is participatory only in the way the assembly line or a hypnotist's blinking flashlight is. Eventually, the conscious mind gives up noting the process and merges with the experience. The body vibrates with the beat and the mind gives itself over, opening up to whatever imagery is offered."

Previously he had described in detail the process of manufacturing an artificial image, which television uses, because never is there a single picture, but many dots being illuminated to form a picture, which changes at a rate faster than the eye can see. A television is an extremely advanced oscilloscope, which can draw thousands of lines a second, where as an oscilloscope can be slowed down to watch the line being drawn.

On page 195 begins the section on hypnosis: "As the largest category of terms that people use to describe their television viewing relates to its hypnotic effect, I asked three prominent psychologists, famous partly for their work with hypnotism, if they could define the TV experience as hypnotic and, if so, what that meant. I described the concrete details of what goes on between viewer and television set: dark room, eyes still, body quiet, looking at light that is flickering in various ways, sound contained to narrow ranges and so on.

"Dr. Freda Morris said, "It sounds like you're giving a course outline in hypnotic trance induction."

"Morris, who is a former professor of medical psychology at UCLA and author of several books on hypnosis, told me that inducing trances was really very easy. The main method is to keep the subject "quiet, still, cut down all diversions and outside focuses," she said, and then to "create a new focus, keep their attention and at a certain point get them to follow your mind.

""There are a great variety of trance states. However, common to all is that the subject becomes inattentive to the enviroment, and yet be very focused on a particular thing, like a bird watching a snake.

""So you mean" I said, "that the goal of the hypnotist is to create a totally clear channel, unencumbered by anything from the outside world, so that the patient can be sort of unified with the hypnotist? She agreed with this way of putting it, adding that hypnotism has power implications which she loathes. ...

"Dr. Ernest Hilgard, who directs Stanford University's research program in hypnosis and is the author of the most widely used texts in the field, agreed that television could easily put people into a hypnotic state if they were ready for it.

"He said that, in his opinion, the condition of sitting still in a dark room, passively looking at light over a period of time, would be the prime component in the induction. "Sitting quietly, with no sensory inputs aside from the screen, no orienting outside the television is itself capable of getting people to set aside ordinary reality, allowing the substitution of some other reality that the set may offer. You can get so imaginatively involved that alternatives temporarily fade away.

...

"Morris said that since television images move more quickly than a viewer can react, one has to chase after them with the mind. This leaves no way of breaking the contact and therefore no way to comment upon the information as it passes in. It stops the critical mind. She told me about an induction technique called "confusion", which was developed by a pioneer in hypnotism, Dr. Milton Erickson. "You give a person so much to deal with that you don't give him a chance to do anything on his own. ... The hypnotist might call the patient's attention to any particular thing, it hardly matters what. Eventually, something like overload is reached, the patient shows signs of breaking and then the hypnotist comes in with some clear relief, some simple instruction, and the patient immediately goes into trance.

"The more I talked with these people, the more I realized how very obvious the process was. Every advertiser, for example, knows that before you can convince anyone of anything, you shatter their existing mental set and then restructure an awareness along lines which are useful to you. You do this with a few very simple techniques like fast-moving images, jumping among attention focuses, and switching moods. There's nothing to it.

Take a look at an advertisement and count the number of scenes in the average ad. It will be found that they average at least ten scenes per commercial, or one every three seconds, and often more than that. They are shifting gears so fast, that you cannot keep up!

On page 200 he comments: "I do not think of myself as hypnotized while watching television. I prefer another frequently used phrase. "When I put on the television, after a while there's the feeling that images are just pouring into me and there's nothing I'm able to do about them."

...

"Since there is no way to stop the images, one merely gives over to them. More than this, one has to clear all channels of reception to allow them in more cleanly. Thinking only gets in the way. ... I noticed how difficult it was to keep mentally alert while watching television. Even so the images kept flowing into me.

"One can never allow oneself to get into such a passive state. Once thinking stops and images begin to flow in, one has surrendered one's mind to the television, and one is never permitted such surrender!"

On page 202 he reports the effect on children: "If television images have any similarity to dream imagery, then this would surely explain a growing confusion between the concrete and the imaginary.

"Television is becoming real to many people while their lives take on the quality of a dream. It would also help explain recent studies, quoted by Marie Winn and many others, that children are showing a decline in reliable memory and in the ability to learn in such a way that articulation and the written word are usable forms of expression.

"For this reason, children should watch but little television, and must be encouraged to do other more creative things, such as reading:

"I asked Peper if he agreed with Krugman that reading was a more active learning process. "Definitely", he said. "Reading produces a much higher amount of beta activity. You would expect abnormality in anyone who produces alpha while reading. The horror of television", he added, "is that the information goes in, but we don't react to it. It goes right into our memory pool and perhaps we react to it later but we don't know what we are reacting to. When you watch television you are training yourself not to react and so later on, you're doing things without knowing why you are doing them or where they came from." (page 211)

He also contends that there is a relationship between television and alcohol abuse (page 213): "Psychiatrists report that an increasing number of people these days complain that they cannot quiet their minds. One cannot will the mind to cease its fixations or ruminations. Even when it comes to sleep or sex or play, experiences that require shifting out of focused thought, the mind continues to churn.

"It is little wonder, therefore, that we have seen a sudden growth of Eastern religious disciplines, ... While many people use these ancient (Satanic) disciplines to achieve freedom from the driving of their minds, most people do not, choosing drugs instead. Alcohol is good. Valium is better. Some sleeping potions work. And there's television.

"They all succeed. Drugs provide escape while passing for experience and relaxation. Television does just as well."

It is far better to spend the time thinking on matters of God, to pray always through meditation and prayer supported by spiritual reading, than to use the Plug-In Drug, as Marie Winn calls the television.

Let us conclude this part of our consideration with a list from page 157 and 158: "If you could somehow drop all preconception of television and read this list as though people were describing some instrument you'd never seen yourself, I think the picture you would obtain is a machine that invades, controls and deadens people who view it. It is not unlike the alien operated "influencing machine" of the psychopathic fantasy.

"1) "I feel hypnotized when I watch television."

"2) "Television sucks my energy."

"3) "I feel like it is brainwashing me."

"4) "I feel like a vegetable when I'm stuck there at the tube."

"5) "Television spaces me out."

"6) "Television is an addiction and I'm an addict."

"7) "My kids look like zombies whem they're watching."

"8) "TV is destroying my mind."

"9) "My kids walk around like they're in a dream because of it."

"10) "Television is making people stupid."

"11) "Television is turning my mind into mush."

"12) "If a television is on, I just can't keep my eyes off of it."

"13) "I feel mesmerized by it."

"14) "TV is colonizing (i.e. taking over) my brain."

"15) "How can I get my kids off it and back into life?"

"At one point I heard my son Kai say: "I don't want to watch television as much as I do but I can't help it. It makes me watch it.""

This may appear extreme, but there are people who from their actions show that they are addicted to television. If any one of these symptoms occur, there is only one cure, pull the plug and walk away from the television. If one is constantly drawn back, as if by a magnet, one must deliver the television to the trash man and be rid of his addiction. However, We believe that there can be moderate use, as there can be moderate use of alcohol, however, there are some who cannot be near a television.

Brainwashing

We have an enemy that desires our eternal damnation, Satan. And he will use every tool available to him. Modern technology has given him a number of new tools. A century and a half ago it was difficult to watch a couple commit fornication. Today you can bring it into your home 24/7 by touching a few buttons on a computer or satellite receiver. It has been said that every advance in video technology came about to serve the porn industry and make vice easier.

The main point is that movies, radio and television are excellent tools to spread the doctrines of devils. Saint Paul says: "Now the Spirit manifestly saith, that in the last times some shall depart from the faith, giving heed to spirits of error, and doctrines of devils,..." [3]

Kennett Bawden, who named the television the satan box noticed in the late 1960's that in a seemingly innocent series in one program they would insert a Communistic message. If one watched carefully, one would notice that they were *paying their dues* to the system of Antichrist. And often the message would be awkwardly inserted. A character would have to act out of character. Later on, though, more messages were inserted and because the characters were becoming more immoral they easily carried off the *message*.

And how many messages does a person miss and take in to their mind, thus polluting it? And messages can be found not only in the last fifty years, but even back in the early days of movies. For instance, I happened to be staying in a friend's home. <u>The Grapes of Wrath</u> was playing on the TV. One of the main characters was talking and his message was quite clear and New Age.

"There were never lacking impious men, nor men who denied God; but were relatively few, isolated and individual, and they did not care or did not think it opportune to reveal too openly their impious mind, as the Psalmist appears to suggest when he exclaims: "The fool hath said in his heart: there is no God." The impious, the atheist, lost in the crowd, denied God, his Creator, only in the secret of his heart. Today, on the contrary, atheism has already spread through large

---

[3]   I Timothy 4:1

masses of the people: well-organized, it works its way even into the common schools; it appears in theaters; in order to spread, it makes use of its own cinema films of the gramaphone and the radio (and television); with its own printing presses it prints booklets in every language; it promotes special exhibitions and public parades; it has formed its own political parties and its own economic and military systems. This organized and militant atheism works untiringly by means of its agitators, with conferences and projections, with every means of propaganda, secret and open, among all classes, in every street, in every hall; it secures for this nefarious activity the moral support of its own universities, and holds fast the unwary with the mighty hands of its organizing power. At the sight of so much activity placed at the service of so wicked a cause, there comes spontaneously to Our mind and Our lips the mournful lament of Christ: "The children of this world are wiser in their generation than the children of light."" Caritate Christi Compulsi, Pope Pius XI

We must remember that the System of Antichrist, run by the various Secret Societies, owns and controls the media, whether it be movies, radio, television, newspapers or magazines. These are all calculated to give honor and glory to Antichrist and serve his goals, not God's!

"There is another explanation for the rapid diffusion of the Communistic ideas now seeping into every nation, great and small, advanced and backward, so that no corner of the earth is free from them. This explanation is to be found in a propaganda so truly diabolical that the world has perhaps never witnessed its like before. It is directed from one common center. It is shrewdly adapted to the varying conditions of diverse peoples. It has at its disposal great financial resources, gigantic organizations, international congresses, and countless trained workers. It makes use of pamphlets and reviews, of cinema, theatre, radio (and television), of schools and even universities. Little by little it penetrates into all classes of the people and even reaches the better-minded groups of the community, with the result that few are aware of the poison which increasingly pervays their minds and hearts." <u>Divini Redemptoris</u>, Pope Pius XI

Pope Pius XI, points out that the cause of the Great Apostasy is to be found in a propaganda so truly diabolical that the world has perhaps never witnessed its like before. "The tools used by the enemy are pamphlets and reviews, of cinema, theatre, radio (and television), of schools and even universities." Since this system uses books, pamphlets, movies, radio and television all in the same manner, the rules for books (Canons 1384-1405) apply equally to the modern inventions of radio, movies and television. There are twelve kinds of books prohibited by the law itself, without need of any other kind of condemnation. [4] Some of these are not only prohibited by Canon Law, but by Divine Law itself.

In 1977 Marie Winn wrote a book called <u>The Plug-In Drug</u> about television: "Television induces a trance like state in the viewer that is the necessary precondition for brainwashing."

Wes Moore wrote an article <u>Television: Opiate of the Masses</u>. [5] Let us consider this:

"An addictive mind control device ... what more could a government or profit-driven corporation ask for? But the really sad thing about television is that it turns everyone into a zombie, no one is immune. There is no higher order of super-intelligent, nefarious beings behind this. It's the product of our very human desire to alter our state of consciousness and excape the hardships of reality.

...

"We're living in a Brave New World, only it is not so brave, or even that new. In fact, it's starting to look more and more like the Dark Ages, with the preliterate zombie masses

---

[4]   These laws are considered in a chapter coming later on.
[5]   http://www.cognitiveliberty.org/5jcl/5JCL59.htm Form <u>The Journal of Cognivitie Liberties</u>, volume 2, issue 2, pages 59-66, 2001 copyright

obeying the authority of the new clergy: Regis Philbin and Jerry Springer."

Now the so-called *Dark Ages* were actually the Ages of Faith, when men and women strived to become saints. What we have today is a truly dark age, which is lighted with the light of a machine that slowly rots away our souls, while we devote most of our free time to it.

How Much Television Do People Watch?

In doing our three week program, we will find out how much television we watch. The numbers have been steadily increasing over the years.

It is hard to find historical data on how much television people watch. In 1956 Bishop Fulton Sheen reported that the average person watched thirty minutes a day. That is three and a half hours a week. Today the average person watch far more than that every day. Let us consider the following from 1992:

> "Most of us (51%) say we watch between seven and 21 hours of TV a week. (People tend to under report their viewing.)" (from Would You Give Up TV For A Million Bucks? TV Guide, October 10, 1992.)

Here is another sign of addiction to television, "(People tend to underreport their viewing.)" It is like asking the problem drinker, "How many drinks have you had?" in all likelihood he or she will lie and give a smaller number of drinks than they have truly had. Only one percent claim to watch over 71 hours per week (seven hours per day); and ten percent claim to watch over 35 hours per week (five hours per day). We can say with certainty, that unless this amount of television is necessary for their employment, they are probably sinning, for their excess curiosity and/or over indulgence in recreation.

Today the average person watches 34 hours per week, which is almost five hours a day. [6] Consider this is almost a full time 40 hour a week job. We sleep 56 hours per week, then work 45 if you add in the commute, then next we spend 34 hours a week with the Satan box. This leaves us only 33 hours a week left for everything else, such as eating, reading, praying, etc. We are spending twenty percent of our time in front of the satan box. How many of us make a Holy Hour once a week, when we should be spending an hour in prayer every day?

Let us consider this from the Cure of Ars, Saint John Vianney: "But if you, dear children, had to pass three or four hours praying in a

---

[6] http://www.tv.com/news/how-much-television-do-you-watch-per-week-24833/

church, as you pass them at a dance or in a cabaret, how heavily the time would press upon you!" [7] Ask the average person to make a Holy Hour once a week and they grumble, but will happily spend more than a day each week enthroned in front of the satan box!

---

[7]   Sermons of the Cure of Ars, page 16

Television Is Addictive

We must first define what an addiction is. An addiction is a habit of sin, which becomes all-consuming and controlling of our life. As such we devote a notable and inordinate amount of time to our addiction. Thus not only alcohol and drugs can be addictive, but also gambling, shopping and many other past times. Addictions tend to be destructive, spiritually, mentally and physically. The spiritual destruction of an addiction is obviously the worst, for addictions are a habit of sin, usually venial, that leads one to weaken and commit mortal sin in some area of their life.

Television and Health Reports:

"Millions of Americans are so hooked on television that they fit the criteria for substance abuse as defined in the official psychiatric manual, according to Rutgers University psychologist and TV-Free America board member Robert Kubey. Heavy TV viewers exhibit five dependency symptoms-- two more than necessary to arrive at a clinical diagnosis of substance abuse. These include: 1) using TV as a sedative; 2) indiscriminate viewing; 3) feeling loss of control while viewing; 4) feeling angry with oneself for watching too much; 5) inability to stop watching; and 6) feeling miserable when kept from watching."

And let us consider this from Television Addiction – A Growing Problem:

"It is noted that the average person spends about three hours a day sitting in front of the TV set, which is half of their leisure time. And, it is known that heavy viewers report watching eight hours a day. The question is, "Are these people addicted to the television?"

"First, let's define an addiction. It is said that addiction is characterized by spending an unusually large amount of time using a substance that is addictive; finding oneself using it more often than intended; thinking about reducing the use, and are making repeated unsuccessful attempts to reduce it; giving up social activities to use the substance, and reporting withdrawal symptoms when one does achieve stopping the use.

"Television can teach and amuse, and it does provide needed distraction and escape. Yet, the difficulty arises when one strongly senses the need to stop viewing as much, and yet find they are unable to reduce viewing." [8]

Note that one definition of an addiction is that we devote a lot of time to it. Let us consider the compulsive gambler. He spends a lot of time at the casino or the race track. And it takes time for an alcoholic to get drunk. We have already seen that the average person spends twenty percent of their time with television, which is excessive. And so on this basis television is addictive.

The Plug-In Drug

In 1977 Marie Winn wrote a book called The Plug-In Drug about television: "And yet the essence of any serious addiction is a pursuit of pleasure."

More recently Wes Moore wrote an article Television: Opiate of the Masses. [9] Let us consider some excerpts from this article.

"That television you watch every day, your secret best friend, is an addictive opiate, and not only that, it's one of the most potent mind-control devices ever produced. And I'm not just basing this on intuition. I have the neurological evidence to prove it.

...

"Of course, not all addictions are chemical. Any behavior that leads to a pleasurable experience will be repeated, especially that behavior requires little work. Psychologists call this pattern "positive enforcement". This is what we mean, technically speaking, by addiction. In this sense, television certainly fits into the category of an addictive agent.

...

---

[8] http://www.allaboutlifechallenges.org/television-addiction.htm

[9]   http://www.cognitiveliberty.org/5jcl/5JCL59.htm Form The Journal of Cognivitie Liberties, volume 2, issue 2, pages 59-66, 2001 copyright

"First of all, when you're watching television the higher brain regions (like the midbrain and the neo-cortex) are shut down, and most activity shifts to the lower brain regions (like the limbic system.) The neurological processes that take place in these regions cannot be accurately be called "cognitive." ... Studies have proven that, in the long run, too much activity in the lower brain leads to atrophy in the higher brain regions."

Let us consider this from a spiritual standpoint. This sounds like we are given ourselves over to our lower nature, which is one of the three enemies we must fight. We must fight the world, the flesh and the devil. And how can we fight the flesh, when we are shutting down that section of our brain that carries on this important fight?

"Televison is like a double edged sword: not only does it cause the endocrine system to release the body's natural opiates (endorphins), but it also concentrates neurological activity in the lower brain regions where we are motivated by nothing but the pursuit of pleasure. Television produces highly functional, mobile "bio-survival robots.""

Some else called these people *sheeple*. When we watch television habitually we make ourselves ready to be led like sheep to the slaughter.

The Evil of Pleasure Seeking

We have seen that watching television causes a release of endorphins, which is a cause of pleasure. And yet we are not created for pleasure, but for happiness. Happiness is a state of being, when our will is in total conformity with the will of Almighty God. Pleasure is a by product of actions, which God grants us. Pleasure is not an end, but merely a byproduct that may or may not occur. Happiness is our true end and can only be found in spiritual things, not material.

Saint Paul warned Timothy (II Tim 3:4) that the people of our time would be: "lovers of pleasure more than of God." And indeed this can be seen to be true in the multiplication of addictions. St. Louis de Montfort says: [10] "Worldlings, on the contrary, rouse one another to persist in their unscrupulous depravity. "Enjoy life, peace, and pleasure," they shout, "Enjoy life, peace and pleasure. Let us eat, let us drink, let us sing, let us dance, let us play. God is good, He did not make us to damn us; God does not forbid us to enjoy ourselves; we shall not be damned for that; away with scruples; we shall not die." And so they continue."

The evil of pleasure seeking can be seen by the condemnation ot two propositions. "Eating and drinking even to satiety for pleasure only, are not sinful, provided this does not stand in the way of health, since any natural appetite can licitly enjoy its own actions." Condemned by Pope Innocent XI (DZ 1158). In other words to eat purely for pleasure is sinful. We should eat to live, not live to eat. If we live to eat, even though it doesn't injure our health, we still are sinfully seeking pleasure.

Pope Innocent XI also condemned the proposition (DZ 1159): "The act of marriage exercised for pleasure only is entirely free of all fault and venial defect." The act of marriage is designed for several purposes,. The primary purposes is the procreation of children. A secondary end is the allaying of concupiscence. Also it is an expression of mutual love. One of these ends must be remotely in mind, when pursuing the act of marriage.

Father Adolphe Tanquerey gives some good advice: [11] "If it be a question of some *pleasure*-passion one must strive to forget the object

---

[10]   Friends of the Cross, page 10
[11]   The Spiritual Life, page 384

of the passion. In order to accomplish this: 1) one must apply the mind and the imagination to any wholesome activity apt to divert attention from the object of passion; one must seek to engage all the powers of the mind on some absorbing object of study, on the solution of some question or problem, or find distraction in play, social intercourse, conversation, walks, etc.... 2) Then, when calm ensues one should have recourse to such moral considerations as may strengthen the will against the allurement of pleasure: considerations of the *natural* order, such as the untoward consequences, for the present and the future, with which a dangerous attachment, a too sentimental friendship may be fraught; but above all one should appeal to the *supernatural* considerations, for instance, that it is impossible to advance in the way of perfection so long as we cling to such attachments., that these are but chains we forge for ourselves, that we thereby risk our salvation, that through our fault scandal may be given, etc."

Let us apply Father Tanquerey's advice to television. Father Schouppe says: "Alas! It is not to the theater that we go to prepare for death!" [12] If one studies the matter well, one must conclude that there are no habitual television viewers in heaven and extremely few in Purgatory. No, most habitual television viewers go straight to hell, for they have weakened their will and in their semi-hypnotic state consented to numerous mortal sins.

And let us consider this well, television is an obstacle to spiritual advancement much more so than any other worldly attachment. Can one see a television in Saint John Vianney's parlor or Saint Vincent Ferrer's? Instead they would rail against it as the satan box, which destroys souls possibly more so than dancing, which Saint John Vianney was vehemently opposed to.

Let us return to Father Tanquerey: "Lastly, *positive acts directly opposed* to the harrassing passion must be elicited." Television leads to worldliness and is a form of worldliness. Meditate on this point. If you do not spend a notable amount of time in meditation, then it is time to get out the shot gun and get rid of the television, for it is keeping you from true prayer!

---

[12]   Hell by Fr. F.X. Schouppe, S.J., page 57

A Code For Catholic Television Viewers

From Parishioner's Handbook

"It is a most pressing need that the conscience of Catholics, with regard to television, should be formed by the sound principles of the Christian Religion." Pope Pius XII (On September 8, 1957 Pope Pius XII issued the now celebrated Encyclical Letter MIRANDA PRORSUS in which he offered the wisest counsel concerning the uses of Television.)

(The Faithful are encouraged to read this great Letter. Available at pamphlet racks and book stores.)

(On February 14, 1958 Pope Pius XII proclaimed St. Clare of Assisi Heavenly Patroness of Television. This great Saint lay gravely ill on Christmas Eve, 1252. Unable to attend Mass she was granted by God the miraculous vision of Mass together with the sound of prayers and music in the Basilica of St. Francis some distance away. For this and other reasons Our Holy Father, granted the often-repeated request made over a period of years by the Faithful, especially by those within the Television industry, and placed this great medium under the Patronage of St. Clare.)

Catholics, in the use of the Television, should -

1. Make thoughtful selection, and profitable use of programs, avoiding those which, whole or in part, might be harmful to Catholic faith or morals, and not accept programs merely on the basis of popularity polls and ratings.

2. Consult the Legion of Decency classification of movies shown on television, as well as reviews and appraisals of other programs, which are published, in Catholic newspapers and periodicals. *Unfortunately the Legion of Decency is no longer available. Do not use secular ratings as they are not reliable.*

3. Use television with due moderation so that viewing practices will not lead to hasty meals, neglect of duty, family conversation, good reading, or discourtesy to guests who may wish neither to view nor to listen.

4. Avoid that late-hour viewing which might lead to damage to health, neglect of night prayers or to morning lateness or unpreparedness for Church, work or school.

5. Control viewing practices so that they will not interfere with attendance at devotions in the Parish church or with regular Confession.

6. Observe moderation in taking or serving intoxicants during viewing, and be mindful of the laws of the Church regarding fast and abstinence.

7. View regularly and attentively Catholic programs which are offered to lead men to perfection of soul, and for the promotion of God's glory furthermore, to encourage others, including non-Catholics, to do likewise. *These programs are no longer available.*

8. Write and send courteous and informative letters of disapproval to both Sponsor and Channel Director when offensive topics, costumes, dances, dialogue, or humor are presented and send letters of appreciation when a program of unusual excellence, by Catholic standards, is presented. Be sure to sign your name, unsigned letters are never recognized.

9 Supervise the viewing practices of the young, and offer correction to statements, etc., when the honor of God and the Church, and the proper moral and mental formation of the children require such correction.

10. See that television (whether with picture or sound only) does not cause children to neglect their religious duties, studies, fresh air, sunshine, exercise, rest, or wholesome companionship, and, finally, that children do not impose their choice of programs against the wishes of their elders.

St. Clare Pray for us

Brief Comments

Above We have commented in *italics*. All need to be extremely careful in regard to television.

The Proper Use of Television

Bishop Hedley says:

"Even when the newspaper is free from objection, it is easy to lose a good deal of time over it. It may be necessary and convenient to know what is going on in the world. But these can be no need of our observing all the rumours, all the guesses and gossip, all the petty incidents, all the innumerable paragraphs in which the solid news appears half-drowned, like the houses and hedges when the floods are out. This is idle and is absolutely bad for brain and character. There is a kind of attraction towards petty and desultory reading of this kind which is sure to leaves its mark on the present generation. The newspapers present not only news, but ideas, reflections, views, inferences and conclusions of every kind.

" ... As the reader takes in all this prepared digested matter he is deluded with the notion that he is thinking and exercising his mind. He is doing nothing of the kind. He is putting on another man's clothes, and fitting himself out with another man's ideas. To do this habitually is to live the life of the child; one is amused and occupied, and one is enabled to talk second-hand talk; but that is all. Men were better men, if they thought at all, in the days when there was less to read. ... Immoderate newspaper reading leads, therefore to much loss of time, and does no good, either to the mind or the heart.

"Most Rev. Dr. Hedley, Bishop of Newport, England, 1881."

In the book Matt Talbot and His Times, the author, Mary Purcell, comments, "Dr. Hedley lived long before the advent of radio and television." Matt Talbot in his spiritual reading had this particular passage marked. Matt Talbot is probably the most notable person to overcome alcoholism through prayer and penance, since the proliferation of whisky. What would Bishop Hedley write today about television and the immoderate use of it, which almost everyone indulges in?

The regulation of television is absolutely essential to salvation. For some, this will mean total abstinence, just as Matt Talbot abstained from alcohol for a large part of his life after indulging in his earlier years.

Secular sources, who consider the problem of television have come up with some rather strict rules. One person advises placing the television in the least desirable room in the house to reduce its attractiveness. Others recommend that there be only one television in the home and no televisions in bed rooms.

The television should be in a cabinet with the doors shut 164 to 168 hours each week. [13] It should not be the focal point of the room. Instead it should take some work to set up to watch television. Consider two centuries ago. How much effort would it be to go to a play? It should take some effort to go and watch television. Television must be a sideline in our life, not a central portion of it. Programs must be chosen with great care. To simply sit there and watch, because you have *nothing better to do* is not the reasoning of a Christian. And television should come after daily Rosary, an hour a day in spiritual reading, meditation and/or contemplation, and other pious practices. We need to learn self-discipline in regard to the television.

Television should be given up in Advent and Lent and on all of the fast days of the Church, such as the Ember Days and certain vigils. In the Ages of Faith the Church forbade plays and other amusements during these holy times. It would be good to give it up at other times, such as on Fridays in honor of the Passion or Saturdays in honor of the Blessed Virgin Mary.

---

[13]   The week is 168 hours long. This would return us to the average viewing when Pope Pius XII wrote his Encyclical on television.

But Television Is Useful and Necessary

Television is a great invention and has a potential for good uses. It is possible with research that some of the damaging effects of television could be eliminated, leaving only its potential for good. So let us look at the positive of television.

Weather

In tornado alley, the television is the best source of information, during a bad storm. Local stations are good about breaking in and giving warnings and going to full time coverage of the more severe storms. Between their spreading of official warnings and the radar one can get a good idea of the danger they are in and take appropriate action. Ever since the first tornado warning was given out in the 1950's, saving a number of people, television has been good in this area. This is one area where radio comes second, being battery powered. The internet has some resources that are also helpful in this type of situation, but not as good as television. We can say that severe weather reporting is the highest and best use of television.

News

"If it bleeds, it leads" is the motto of news. What is the true purpose of news? News should provide us with the information we need to discharge our responsibilities in life. Now, knowing about a sensational murder case is not only not necessary, but often a sin of gossip and curiosity. And so this type of news is a waste of time.

And look at the national news. In the United States, the President is good for three to five minutes a night. When Obama was elected several nights were devoted to a discussion of the dog he was going to get his kids, while in the White House. Hardly necessary for us to know. And on a slow news day, one can see something as inane as President's Dog Does Duty on White House Lawn. The only time the President got pushed aside was when Vice President Dick Cheney had his *friendly fire incident* in a hunting accident, when he accidentally shot someone. Because we must vote, there are things we need to know about our politicians, but the network news is notoriously bad at supplying this information. Since the invention of the internet far more useful information can be found there and quicker than devoting a half an hour every night to the national news.

And there is another drawback to news. The stories are usually incomplete. In the late 1990's I heard a piece of information, I thought would be useful, so I wrote it down. Over the next two years I made other notes. Someone asked my opinion on these things, so I went through my notes and organized them. It had taken me two years to get a fairly good picture. Now, if I wish to update this information, I can do it in a few minutes on the internet. I have noticed this incompleteness in newspapers as well. Stop and think, are there any questions left unanswered?

Today there are far better sources of information than television.

Improvement Programming

There are several times of improvement programs. There are cooking shows and do it yourself shows for household projects. Used in moderation, these may provide useful information. The various medical and psychological shows, however should be avoided. One popular medical show encourages the mortal sin of using condoms. Other shows promote acceptance of sinful life styles.

Religious Programming

Saint Clare was named patron saint of television, because she miraculously was able to assist at Mass by seeing it from a distance. If this were possible today, this would be a good use of television, providing Mass for those unable to assist at it. However, this is not available. All such programming promotes the spirit of Vatican II, which is the spirit of Antichrist. [14]

---

[14] For more information see my book 54 Years that Changed the Catholic Church

Curiosity Is a Sin

The Baltimore Catechism says: "See, then, what caused Eve's sin. She went into the dangerous occasion, and was admiring the forbidden fruit when the tempter came. She listened to him, yielded to his wicked suggestions, and sinned." Ever since Eve looked at the apple and listened to the serpent, we have been in trouble. Original sin came from a sin of curiosity, which was committed by Eve and then Adam.

Our mind is like to a computer, which is constantly receiving information from our five senses. It is also processing this information for use later on, as well as storing it. If it receives bad information, then it can produce a bad output, that is sin. Consider, a boy who sees a naked young woman. Will he ever be able to forget that image, which has been stored in his mind? Might this image return to his mind a half a century later, when he is on his death bed and cause his damnation? "The unhappy soul will then say: Had I mortified myself by not looking at such an object; ... if I had read a spiritual book every day;" [15] How many of us are taking in information that is worthless? How many of us are taking in information that is down right perverse, and excusing it as mere *entertainment*? There is no excuse for sin. We have an intellect and will and it is our duty to keep our intellect pure.

Sacred Scripture says:

"In unnecessary matters be not over curious, and in many of His works thou shalt not be inquisitive." [16]

"And many of them who had followed curious arts brought together their books and burnt them before all. And, counting the price of them, they found the money to be fifty thousand pieces of silver." [17]

At current silver prices, this would be a million dollars with of bad books that were burnt.

---

[15] St. Alphonsus: <u>Preparation For Death</u>, page 285
[16]   Ecclesiasticus 3:24
[17]   Acts 19:19

When we think of curiosity, we have been told that it is a good thing to be encouraged, not a sin to be avoided. Saint Thomas Aquinas distinguishes between the virtue of studiousness and the vice of curiosity in his Summa Theologica.

Father Tanquerey says: "Curiosity is a disease of the mind, which is one of the causes of religious ignorance, for it leads us to seek too eagerly the knowledge of things that delight us rather than of things that are profitable to us, and thus to lose precious time." [18]

Let us look at a book, The Devil:

"Now, dear readers, we must conclude. The misfortunate of most men is that they know not how to conclude. They hear a discourse, they read a book, **and go to their business, or their pleasures without having asked themselves: "What is the result of this is relation to my personal conduct?"** If you are reading this out of mere curiosity, then this paper is worthless to you, you must ask yourself: What is the warning that Providence now gives me?" [19]

And this is how we should seek information. We should seek it for our good, spiritual and material. Pope Pius XI says: "Similarly the sustained effort to understand supernatural things excites men to live more perfectly." This is why we are recommending an hour a day in spiritual pursuits in addition to our other devotions. We need this concentrated time in order to live more perfectly.

Henry Edward Cardinal Manning warns:

"Curiosity and recklessness fascinate thousands to their fall. The want or the loss of the gift of science, which as a sensitive instinct turns away from error as you would turn away from evil, causes even good minds to go astray. Sometimes they lose the delicate perception of what is true and the delicate horror of what is false. Take care, then, of what books you read, of what friends you make, of what

---

[18]   The Spiritual Life, page 387
[19]   Pages 174-6 (Emphasis mine)

conversations you indulge in, of everything that can cloud the light and discernment of faith that is within you." [20]

We should add that what we take in by way of radio, television and the internet has a similar danger.

Saint Bernard says:
"Some there are who desire knowledge merely for the sake of knowing, and this is shameful curiosity ... and some there are who desire knowledge that they may put their knowledge up for sale for gain or for honors, and this is disgraceful trafficking: but some there are who desire knowledge that they may edify others, and this is charity: and finally, there are some who desire knowledge that they may thereby be edified themselves, and this is prudence."

And Saint Augustine says: "We are forbidden to be curious: and this is a great gift that temperance bestows." We must be studiousness seeking knowledge in order to better ourselves, spiritually and material and to serve our neighbor in his needs and wants.

Let us close with this thought from Blessed Anna-Maria Taigi:
"God will send two punishments: one will be in the form of wars, revolutions and other evils; it shall originate on earth. The other will be sent from Heaven. There shall come over the whole earth an intense darkness lasting three days and three nights. Nothing can be seen, and the air will be laden with pestilence which will claim mainly, but not only, the enemies of religion. It will be impossible to use any man-made lighting during this darkness, except blessed candles. He, who out of curiosity, opens his window to look out, or leaves his home, will fall dead on the spot. During these three days, people should remain in their homes, pray the Rosary and beg God for mercy."

During the Three Days of Darkness, which comes at the end of the current period of Catholic Church history, the Great Apostasy,

---

[20]   Internal Mission of the Holy Ghost page 314

anyone who looks outside will have this curiosity punished by death. [21] We are living in the Age of Curiosity, and this curiosity has led to enumerable sins.

Let us consider this warning from the Blessed Virgin Mary at Quito Ecuador, speaking of our times:

> "The third meaning of the lamp's going out is that those times the air will be filled with the spirit of impurity which like a deluge of filth will flood the streets, squares and public places. The licentiousness will be such there will be no more virgin souls in the world."

Virginity is more than bodily virginity. It requires also virginity of the heart and soul. With the introduction of television this prophecy has been literally fulfilled. Consider the filth currently being broadcast through the air waves by radio, television and satellites. The air is literally filled with impurity. With a little receiver we can tap into the most vile things easily. And today, there are no virgin souls. All have been exposed to evils they should not have been and at the most tender of ages.

"Contemplation," says St. Peter of Alcantara, "cannot endure curiosity, whether of the senses or of the mind. . . . All this takes up time, disturbs the senses, disquiets and dissipates the soul, and scatters it in all directions." And all reasonable people are created for contemplation. By reasonable people we mean all who have the use of reason. Therefore the only ones not created for contemplation are infants, who are not yet ready for contemplation, and the perpetually insane. Once we reach the age of reason we begin our journey towards contemplation, which is our goal in life. We can see that curiosity keeps us from our goal of reaching divine contemplation.

---

[21]   For more information, please see my book The Coming Chastisement.

Watching Television Can Be a Sin

Watching television can be a sin. It should be obvious that to watch immoral television is a sin, but the quantity of television watched can also be sinful. In and of itself to watch habitually three or more hours a day is a venially sinful habit of waste of time. Watching a three hour movie every six months would not be a sin, but to do this day in and day out is certainly sinful.

Also there are certain other habits in regard to television viewing that are sinful. And the first of these is to go to bed with television. Our last thought before going to sleep should be a pious thought and television rarely produces such thoughts. We should close the day with our night prayers and preparation of the next day's meditation not with the TV.

Also late night viewing can be a sin against charity, for the radio and television both disturb the peace and quiet that should reign in a home after bed time until after morning prayers.

Television viewing can become a mortal sin, when it leads to a major neglect of our responsibilities to Almighty God, our neighbor especially our family and our self.

There is one sin in regard to radio, television and even texting that must be addressed. This is the mortal sin of blasphemy, which is so prevalent in the world today. We ask God's forgiveness in advance for using the following example from the world of texting and the internet. OMG is used to express astonishment and according to the internet it does not mean Oh My Goodness. It is an act of blasphemy. You may say, but I mean Oh My Goodness, when I use it. Saint Paul says: "But prove all things; hold fast that which is good. From all appearance of evil refrain yourselves." [22] We cannot use anything with a *double meaning* like this. To use something with a double meaning like this is an act of scandal as it may lead others into sin because them believe it means something else from what we intend.

And blasphemy can be found in the world of television. In fact using the above phrase was the trait of a co-star on a series from thirty years ago. [23] He would say this about once an episode. And thus that series must be condemned as mortally sinful for the blasphemy. It is not sufficient to adopt the habit of making an act of reparation every time a blasphemy is heard. That is fine in the world, where we cannot avoid contact with mortal sinners, but for *entertainment* we must be stricter. If we do hear a blasphemy in a news report or elsewhere, we should make an act of reparation. If we find it in our *entertainment* it is time to flip the television off. To fail to do so is to cooperate in the sin. This cooperation is more evil that watching a pornographic movie! And this is an area where many have relaxed. They have come to accept blasphemy as simply something we must live with. And this is a danger with television. By habitually viewing evil we come to accept it.

Many other things can be said on the sinfulness of television, but this would make this book larger than it needs to be. We have discussed the promotion of divorce and homosexuality. All theologians agree that every sin against the sixth and ninth commandments is mortal. And this includes all *off color* jokes and stories or any discussion of any immoral act, no matter how obliquely it is discussed. Many Moral Theology books go into Latin when they must discuss the various sins a priest may hear in Confession to show how series this matter is. [24] Many televisions cross the line into immorality in this manner. Remember if it is a sin to do it, it is a sin to talk about it or even think about it. Therefore it is a sin to watch anything which discusses it.

---

[22]   I Thessalonians 5:21-22
[23]   <u>Magnum PI</u>
[24]   Priests must know these things, and therefore are permitted to study them as a necessary near occasion of sin. However, they are warned to be careful and not exceed the requirements of duty.

Moral Television

It is nearly impossible to go through the television show by show and condemn those that are immoral. There is a story told of a mother in the early 1970's, who wanted to check movies before she allowed her children to go. So she would go to the movie and watch it first. After a month or two she realized that she was wasting her time, because she hadn't found a decent movie yet. The same can be said of much that is on television.

And so we have gone back over the television we recall watching before we gave it up entirely and made a list of those series that never crossed the line into immorality. The list is in the empty box above. Actually that is an exaggeration, but the list is rather short. Antiques Roadshow has never crossed the line in the episodes I watched. Also Extreme Homes never crossed the line. As I recall This Old House didn't.

Although I was an avid viewer of Jeopardy it did cross the line by spreading false propaganda. True, I would sit there and correct them, but one cannot recommend a program that habitually teaches error. Our minds are created for truth and we should only allow the truth to enter our minds.

And many programs promote the false ideals of the world today. Let us look at the homosexual agenda, which may soon lead to nationwide legitimation of homosexual unions as *marriages*. Just as the Supreme Court legalized murder of the unborn, they may soon force homosexuality upon us. This Supreme Court consists today of six nominal Catholics, who are not doing their duty to promote morals as required by the Natural Law. And this softening in regard to homosexuality has come from all forms of television. Take a look at an innocent sounding program, House Hunters. How many *couples* are homosexuals seeking a new home in which to commit sin? In fact many other couples are what the Census Bureau calls POSLQs, that is persons of the opposite sex sharing living quarters. As Catholics we call it *living in sin*. Just as we cannot do it, we should not participate in it in any way, even on television. In fact, to watch such a program is certainly sinful. Is it possibly a mortal sin of cooperation in the sin of another? We recall being sickened by a cooking competition series. One of the participants bragged about how proud her *partner* of the same sex would be at her progress in learning to cook. We did not watch that one ever again. Although those episodes which do not promote some form of immorality are acceptable, we should consider refraining from those as well. We need to *vote with our feet* and avoid promoting such programs.

Saint Paul says: "But prove all things; hold fast that which is good. **From all appearance of evil refrain yourselves.**" [25] By watching an immoral program we are giving scandal and a bad example.

We have seen how evil can be found in seemingly innocent places. Consider a sporting event. How many times have the announcers gotten off into immorality, because the action on the field was boring and they just started talking? And let us not forget immodesty in dress, which is rampant in the world today. We may not be able to avoid it on the street, but we must not invite it into our living room.

Take a look at the Ten Commandments. If it is a sin to do it, it is likewise a sin to watch it on television. We must be very careful, because it is so easy to cross the line into sinfulness and the habitual television viewer will eventually cross the line.

The Legion of Decency condemned <u>Miracle on 34th Street</u> - condemned because of its sympathies toward a divorced mother, played by Maureen O'Hara. [26] Any series, which portrays a divorced person should be avoided, for this is promoting divorce. Canon 1399, which is reproduced below, forbids anything immoral, including anything that promotes divorce.

Much more could be written, but it is time that we made wise choices in regard to television and were critical of everything. And the choice to leave the television off must always be an option. And we

---

[25]   I Thessalonians 5:21-22
[26] http://en.wikipedia.org/wiki/List_of_films_condemned_by_the_Legion_of_Decency

should not admit anything into our homes that we would not allow a child to watch, unless it is absolutely necessary. The news is permitted, provided it does not cross the line and there is some necessity of watching it.

Some shows must be condemned in part, because they indulge in gossip and detraction. Even the news does this, so we must be careful here. We have been taught that we have a right to know everything, and this is simply not true. Detraction is the unjust revelation of the sins of another. Let us take the revelation of President Clinton's violations of the eighth commandment, which served to be the topic on the news for some months. One result was that a whole generation was taught new ways to violate the eighth commandment!

And we must examine our conscience carefully. Have I watched television programs or movies that are immoral? The answer is most likely that I have. I must repent of my sin and go now and sin no more. This is the choice. And a good penance would be to abstain from television for a notable amount of time. We must also ask ourselves if television has caused us to lower our standards? As programs got worse are there programs that I would not watch when they first came out, but now watch in reruns?

The Satan Box

Tertullian reports:

"You, have nothing to do with a sacred place which is tenated by such multitudes of diabolic spirits."

"That immodesty of gesture and attire which so specially and peculiarly characterizes the stage are consecrated to them-the one deity wanton by her sex, the other by his drapery; while its services of voice, and song, and lute, and pipie, belong to Apollos, and Muses, and Minervas, and Mercuries."

"Nay, as regards the arts, we ought to have gone further back, and barred all further argument by the position that the demons, predetermined in their own interests from the first, among other evils of idolatry, the pollutions of the public shows, with the object of drawing man away from his Lord and binding him to their own service, carried out their purpose by bestowing on him the artistic gifts which the shows require."

In <u>De Spectaculis</u> Tertullian devotes a whole chapter to satanic influence and the theater. More recently an organization has released a DVD, <u>Hollywood Unmasked</u>, which reports the satanic influence upon Hollywood, movies and television. [27] This DVD has numerous quotes from actors about how they have let themselves be influenced by Satan. Basically they step out of the way and let satan possess them to improve their acting ability. Obviously such a practice cannot be permitted or cooperated in in any manner whatsoever.

"There are television sets in every home, every restaurant, every hotel room, and every shopping mall— now they're even small enough to carry in your pocket like electronic rosaries. It is an unquestioned part of everyday life. Kneeling before the cathode-ray

---

[27] We should warn all that this DVD contains some shocking things. One of the most shocking is the one they do not comment on. They have a clip from a popular *sitcom*, which denigrates going to church. In the clip one of the actors commits a blasphemy and they so not say a word about it. We cannot recommend watching this DVD.

god, with our TV Guide concordance in hand, we maintain the illusion of choice by flipping channels (chapters and verses)." [28] This was written in 1992 by the founder of the Church of Satan, Anton LaVey. He also wrote The Satanic Bible, as a guide book for ushering in a new Age of Satan.

LaVey continues: "... The birth of TV was a magical event foreshadowing its satanic significance. The first commercial broadcast was aired on Walpurgisnacht, April 30th, 1939, at the New York World's Fair. Since then, TV's infiltration has been so gradual, so complete that no one even noticed. People don't need to go to church any more; they get their morality plays on television." [29]

Let us consider this last point. Let us look at how morals have been degraded on television since its introduction after World War II. There have been several shifts towards immorality in the past two thirds of a century. The 1960's saw the introduction of the continued story of the sins of Peyton Place. This assisted in lowering morals and introduced many to the habit of watching people live in a continual state of mortal sin. And then the late 1970's saw Roots and a host of mini-series, which also depicted many sins and introduced people to many things we should not know, such as gang rape in jails, for instance. The 1980's saw the advent of cable and satellite television, which allowed people to bring in even worse things, since there were some restrictions on broadcast television.

Anton LaVey predicted: "We can use TV as a potent propaganda machine. The stage is set for the infusion of true satanic philosophy and potent (emotionally inspiring) music to accompany the inverted crosses and pentagrams." [30] And let us look at 2011. How many prominent people are living a life of sin? promote the homosexual agenda? Indeed television has softened the thinking of everyone who watches it regularly. It truly can be called the satan box.

---

[28] Anton LaVey, The Devil's Notebook (Portland, Oregon, Feral House, 1992), p.84.
[29] Ibid. p. 86.
[30] The Devil's Notebook, page 85 Anton LaVey

Prayer and Television

It should be obvious that radio and television must be turned off during prayer time, but some have forgotten even that. Many have forgotten the requirements for true prayer.

Prayer must be attentive, persevering, reverential, humble, trustful and offered up for things necessary or useful to salvation. Voluntary distraction in prayer is sinful because irreverent. A set form of words is not prayer at all if we have not external attention, that is, if we are engaged in doing what is absolutely incompatible with internal attention of even the most tenuous kind." <u>Moral and Pastoral Theology</u>, Davis, Volume II, pages 7 and 8.

Since attention is opposed to distraction, external attention is that which excludes distractions, viz. all those external acts which occupy a person to such extent that he is no longer able to attend to the meaning of his prayer. Thus, for instance, external attention would be lacking if during prayer a man reads, or paints, or watches television, or does some other work which requires keen attention; on the other hand, external attention is present if he prays while he walks or performs some light work which does not require much attention. (Such as sweeping or scrubbing the floor, weeding the garden, digging a ditch, etc.) Such external attention well deserves to be called attention since a person is thus applying himself to prevent his prayer being disturbed by external occupations. (such as watching television) For just as a man who takes care that no wild animals wander into his flower garden is said to be attending his garden, so in the same way a man who turns aside from external occupations is attending to his prayer. <u>Moral Theology</u>, Prummer, page 171.

A voluntary distraction is sinful, because it is irreverent, that is it is willfully placing an obstacle between us and God. An involuntary distraction is not irreverent, because it is not willed, in fact one can pray even if distracted involuntarily the whole time. Now is the leaving of the television on during prayer and spiritual reading a sinful distraction?

Television and the Divine Office

Question: In the series of articles on the Divine Office, which appeared some months ago in the pages of The Homiletic and Pastoral Review, the explanation of the attention required for the recitation of the Office led me to wonder a bit. How about those who attempt to recite the work of God (Divine Office) in front of a television set, watching a ball game, or while listening to the radio? If one would do this, would he satisfy his obligation, or would he fail in his duty

(signed) FRATER

Answer: Basically, the answer to Frater's question must be found in the rule set down in that very article.

"The minimum requirement for validly satisfying the precept is that there be external attention. This means that the cleric is not performing any other action which is incompatible with internal attention. In this respect, much depends upon how serious an impediment the other action is."

It seems quite clear that one could fail to satisfy the obligation of the canonical hours (or other prayer) while watching a television program, even intermittently, because he would fail to give the required attention to the Divine Office. ...

However, our consideration of this matter should not be limited to the valid fulfillment of the obligation. One who is satisfied merely with this is falling short of what is expected of him and of what is his duty. Speaking of the priest and the Divine Office, our Holy Father, Pope Pius XII, sets forth the attitude that every cleric should have toward the recitation of the canonical hours.

"The Divine Office is a most efficacious means of sanctification. Certainly it is not a mere recitation of formularies or of artistically executed chants; it is not just a question of respect for certain norms, called rubrics, or for external ceremonies of worship; it is above all a matter of elevating the mind and heart to God, in unison with the blessed spirits, who eternally sing praises to God. Therefore, the canonical hours should be recited worthily, attentively, and with devotion, as we are reminded at the beginning of the Office."

We should remember that the will of God is our sanctification. And does television sanctify us?

Having thus described the recitation of the canonical hours, our Holy Father addresses to all priests an admonition that cannot be put into practice who seeks or who willfully admits distracting influences during his recitation of the Divine Office. The Supreme Pontiff exhorts:

"Meditate with care and attention on these fertile truths which the Holy Ghost has disclosed to us in the Sacred Scriptures, and upon which the writings of the Fathers and Doctors are commentary explanations. As your lips repeat the words dictated by the Holy Ghost, try not to lose anything of this great treasure, and, that your souls may be responsive to the grace of God, put away from your minds with all effort and zeal whatever might distract you, and recollect your thoughts, that you may thus more easily and with greater fruit attend to the contemplation of the eternal truths." Homiletic and Pastoral Review, pages 833, 834, volume 54, June, 1954.

What is said here of the Divine Office applies to spiritual reading, meditation, private prayer, the Rosary, etc. It is impossible to pray properly in front of a television that is on, even if the sound be off. The television is a voluntary distraction. Before beginning spiritual reading or prayer of any sort the television must be turned off completely.

St. Thomas states (II-II, Q83, A13): "Purposely to allow one's mind to wander in prayer is sinful and hinders the prayer from having fruit. It is against this that Augustine says in his Rule: "When you pray God with psalms and hymns, let your mind attend to that which your lips pronounce." But to wander in mind unintentionally does not deprive prayer of its fruit."

What Is More Important?

In analyzing how we spend our time, let us ask several questions.

First how much time do we spend with Almighty God? We can count all of the time devoted to prayer, meditation, contemplation and spiritual reading.

Next add up the amount of time we spend with television. And so what is more important, God or the television? Most of us must answer that television is four to ten times more important to us than Almighty God, and this must change if we hope to save our souls.

And we can also do this in other areas of our life. For instance, how much does a mother or father spend with their spouse and with their children?

Studies report that if we made a list of the time we use, sleep would come first, then work and then television. Whereas we spend a whole day or more with television each week, many can't be bothered to spend more than a few minutes with the family. We must conclude, if we are honest, that television takes far too much of our time. It's use must be greatly curtailed, if not eliminated.

Should I Give Up Television Entirely?

If you balk at even thinking of giving up television entirely, then you probably should give it up, at least for a notable amount of time. Television is incompatible with the spirit of fasting of penitential seasons, such as Advent and Lent, so going without television for a complete Lent, including Sundays, is advisable for all who want to go to heaven.

Let us consider the 1957 Franciscan Third Order Rule:

> "They shall steadfastly avoid dances, theatrical performances, films and television shows that tend to be offensive to good morals, and also all forms of dissipation. Concerning dances in general, tertiaries shall observe exactly the regulations laid down by the Church in their various localities, so that they may never be the cause of scandal. To put the spirit of penance into practice better and to foster recollection, it is to be recommended that they abstain altogether from dances, theatrical performances, films and television shows."

To give up television is certainly being recommended here. Let us ask the opposite question: "Is it a sin to give up television?" The answer would be no, it is not a sin.

Let us consider Pope Pius XII's to Instruction to Lenten Preacher's given in 1944, which is of great value to our consideration here, and upon which We shall comment:

> "A fact which always repeats itself in the history of the church is that when faith and Christian morals clash with strong adverse currents of error or vitiated appetites, attempts are made to overcome the difficulties with some sort of easy compromise, or otherwise to side-step and elude them."

The road to hell is paved with compromise with evil, which is NEVER permitted.

Pope Pius XII next points out that many try to compromise with evil by trying to find an expedient way to conform the Commandment with evil, but such is not possible.

> "Who does not see how in the clear knowledge that a determined human act is against the Commandment of God, it is implied that it cannot be directed to the end of union with Him, precisely because it contains the aversion, that is, the estrangement of the soul, from God and His will (aversio a Deo fine ultimo), an aversion which destroys union and friendship with Him, which is, precisely, the hallmark of grave sin? When man says "Yes" to the forbidden fruit, he says "No" to the prohibiting God; when he puts himself and his will before God and divine will; aversion to God and the intimate essence of grave sin consist in this."

Not Thy will but my will is the road to hell. This is why We choose Fiat voluntas Tua (Thy will be done), because God's will is the road to heaven, and our will the road to hell.

> St. Paul reminds us, ""If (according to man) I fought with beasts at Ephesus, what doth it profit it me, if the dead not rise again? Let us eat and drink, for to-morrow we shall die. Be not seduced: Evil communications corrupt good manners. Awake ye just, and sin not. For some have not the knowledge of God, I speak it to your shame." (I Corinthians 15:32-34)

And let us remember that much of what is broadcast on television and radio is corrupting and must be avoided.

Church Pronouncements on Radio, Movies and Television

The Church has not said a great deal on these subjects, since these inventions are new. In the next section we will see what the Fathers of the Church and the Saints had to say about theater, because television is nothing other than a *home theater*.

In 1954 Pope Pius XII wrote an Apostolic Letter, "The rapid advances which television has now made in many countries keeps Our attention ever more alert to this marvelous gift of science and technology, at once precious and dangerous by reason of the profound reverberations which it is destined to provoke in the private and public life of nations. We fully recognize the value of this brilliant conquest of science, which is a further manifestation of the wonderful splendors of God, Who "has given science to men that He may be honored in its marvels." Television too, therefore, imposes on all of us the duty of gratefulness which the Church tirelessly recommends to her children in the daily Holy Sacrifice of the Altar, with the admonition that "it is truly meet and just, right and salutary, always and everywhere to give thanks" to God for His gifts.

"In any case, it is not difficult to realize the innumerable advantages of television whenever it is placed at the service of man for his perfection.

"In recent years, the movies and sports, to say nothing of the necessity of daily work, have tended to draw the members of the family increasingly away from home, upsetting the natural development of domestic life. How can We not rejoice to see television efficaciously contributing to the restoration of balance, offering the whole family the chance of enjoying together pleasant recreation far from the dangers of unhealthy company and places? How can We be indifferent to the beneficent influence which television is able to exercise from the social point of view in respect to culture, popular education, scholastic teaching, and the very life of peoples, who through that instrument will certainly be helped to know and to understand one another better and to reach friendly concord and better mutual co-operation.

"Such considerations, however, must not blind us to another aspect of this delicate and important question. Although, in face, television properly controlled may constitute an effective means of wise and Christian education, it is equally true that it is not exempt from dangers which may be the result of abuses and profanation brought about by human weakness and malice-dangers all the more serious since the suggestive power of this instrument is greater and the public toward whom it is directed is wider and more indiscriminate. Unlike the theater and the movies, whose spectacles are limited to those who choose to enter, television is directed above all, to family groups of every age and sex and of various cultural levels, bringing to them the daily news, sundry news items, and all kinds of spectacles. Like the radio, it can enter any house and go to any place at any time, bringing with it not only sounds and words but also the concreteness and mobility of its images, which gives it greater emotional influence, particularly in respect to the young. To this must be added the fact that television programs are based, in great part, on films and plays, which, as experience has shown, all too frequently do not satisfy the requirement of natural and Christian ethics. Lastly, it should be pointed out that television finds its keenest and most attentive audience among children and adolescents, who, by reason of their age can more easily fall prey to its fascination and, consciously or unconsciously, transmute into living reality the images they absorb from the animated picture on the screen. It is obvious, therefore, how intimately television affects the education of the young and the Christian spirit of the family.

"If we consider the inestimable value of the family, which is the primary cell of society, and if We reflect that within the walls of the home not only the bodily but also the spiritual development of the child must begin and grow-precious hope of the Church and of its country-We cannot but proclaim to all those who share the responsibilities of television that the duties and responsibilities which rest on their shoulders are extremely serious before God and society.

"Public authorities above all, must take every precaution, so that the atmosphere of decency and restraint which should surround family life may not be offended or troubled.

"Ever present in Our mind is the sad picture of the perturbing and evil power of the movies. But how can We help being horrified by the thought that through television the poisoned atmosphere of materialism, superficiality, and luxuriousness, which too often pervades the motion picture theaters, may penetrate the walls of the home? Truly, it would be impossible to imagine anything more fatal to spiritual forces of a nation than that, before so many innocent souls, in the bosom of the family itself, there should be repeated those sensational revelations of pleasure-seeking, of passion, and of evil which can shake and ruin for all time a whole edifice of purity, goodness, and healthy individual and social education.

"For these reasons, We deem it advisable to point out that the normal supervision which has to be exercised by the authorities responsible for public shows is not sufficient, in the case of television transmissions, to ensure satisfactory service from the moral point of view; there is a need for a different criterion, as it is here a question of spectacles destined to reach into the family sanctuary.

"Thus we see, particularly in this field, that there is no foundation in the supposed right to indiscriminate liberty in art and the plea that thought and the imparting of information are free; higher values are at stake, the violators of which would not be able to escape the heavy penalties threatened by the divine Saviour, "Woe to the world because of scandals! ... Woe to the man by whom the scandal cometh!"

"We cherish a profound trust that the lofty sense of responsibility of those who preside over public life will prevail in prevention of those sad possibilities which We have previously deplored. We are pleased to hope, rather, that as far as the programs are concerned, suitable instructions will be issued, so that television may serve the healthy recreation of the citizens and likewise contribute in all circumstances to their education and moral elevation. But in order that such desirable measure may find their full application, a careful and active vigilance will have to be exercised by all." Pope Pius XII, Apostolic Letter, January 1, 1954

Since the public authorities have completely failed, We remind everyone of Our Predecessors last admonition: "But in order that such desirable measure may find their full application, a careful and active vigilance will have to be exercised by all." Unfortunately television has become such a pervayer of filth, that extra vigilance is required. To determine our duty We shall consult Church pronouncements on books, radio and movies, which can be applied to the *home theater.*

In 1947 Pope Pius XII said, "The radio can be one of the most powerful means for spreading true civilization and culture. Today its services have become almost indispensable for educating men in the sense of solidarity, for the life of the State and the people; it is capable of creating a lively force of cohesion in peoples and between nations. It can bear witness before the whole world to the truth and glory of God, promote the victory of equity, bring light, consolation, hope, reconciliation, and love on this earth, and draw men and nations closer together. It can carry the voice of Christ, the truth of the Gospel, the spirit of the Gospel, and the charity of the Gospel to the ends of the earth. It gives also to Us, common Father of the faithful, the joy of being, at one and the same time, present to all Our children in the whole world, every time We send out our messages and impart Our blessing.

"All this the radio can do. But in the hands of blind or wicked men it can also lend itself to error and falsehood, base passions, sensuality, pride, covetousness, and hate; it can be turned into that open sepulcher full of malediction and bitterness of which St. Paul speaks and which swallows up the Christian virtues, sound civilization, peace, and human happiness. ...

"At the service of the dignity of life and Christian ethics: It should hold sacred the child's innocence, and youth's purity, the holy chastity of matrimony, and the happiness of a family life based on the fear and love of God.

"At the service of justice: It should hold sacred the invioable human rights no less than the right of the authorities to exact from the individual and the community the duties necessary for the common good; the right of peoples to existence, in particular of the weaker members, and alike the right of the great family of nations to request the sacrifices necessary for the peace of the world; the right of the church to bring, in the fullness of liberty, to all men and all peoples the wealth of the grace and peace of Christ.

"At the service of love: This is the duty of the present hour. At all costs it is necessary to overcome dissension and hate, of which the radio, too, has many times been made the instrument and agent. May it put its far-reaching powerful influence to the service of the noble ideal of Christian charity. ...

"Finally, We wish to draw attention to the understanding of the true needs of humanity and its spiritual nature, which the radio should serve by its musical transmissions. We have no intention of speaking now of those programs in which it would be very difficult to find any artistic merit, any educational value. ... Rather, We refer to the recital of sacred music, as well as to the efforts to make accessible to the public the works, sacred and profane, of the great modern and ancient composers, whose masterpieces arouse in the mind and soul the lofty sentiments by which they were themselves animated." Address to the Congress of the 50th Anniversary of the Convezione Marcioniane Radio, October 3, 1947

Pope Pius XII states that the radio can become an open sepulcher. Television has far exceeded radio in becoming an open sepulcher of the most vile rottenness! And in another place he says:

"One wonders at times if the leaders of the motion picture industries fully appreciate the vast power they wield in affecting social life, whether in the family or the larger civil groups. The eyes and ears are like broad avenues that lead directly to the soul of man; and they are opened wide, most often without challenge, by the spectators of your films. What is it that enters from the screen into the inner recesses of the mind, where youth's fund of knowledge is growing and where norms and motives of conduct that will mold the definitive character are being shaped and sharpened? Is it something that will contribute to the formation of a better citizen, industrious, law-abiding, God-fearing, who finds his joy and recreation in wholesome pleasure and amusement? St. Paul was quoting Meander, an ancient Greek poet, when he wrote to the faithful of his church in Corinth that "bad conversation corrupts good manners." What was true then is no less true today; because human nature changes little with the centuries. And if it is true, as it is, that bad conversation corrupts morals, how much more effectively are they corrupted by bad conversation when accompanied by conduct, vividly depicted, which flouts the laws of God and civilized decency? Oh, the immense amount of good the motion picture can effect! This is why the evil spirit, always so active in this world, wishes to pervert this instrument for his own impious purposes; and it is encouraging to know that your committee is aware of the danger, and more and more conscious of its grave responsibility before society and God. It is for public opinion to sustain wholeheartedly and effectively every legitimate effort made by men of integrity and honor to purify the movies and keep them clean, to improve them and increase their usefulness." July 14, 1945 Pope Pius XII Address to United States Movie Producers

How many eyes and ears sit hours in front of the television, like broad avenues that lead directly to the soul of man; and they are opened wide, most often without challenge, by the spectators of your films, and programs? How many shall find that their eyes and ears shall burn in hell for the sins committed by improper use of the television and other media?

In 1955 Pope Pius XII described the ideal film, "The first quality which should mark the ideal film is respect for man. For there is indeed no reason whereby it can be exempted from the general norm which demands that he who deals with men should fully respect man. However much difference of age, condition, and sex may suggest a difference in conduct and bearing, man is always man, with the dignity and nobility bestowed on him by the Creator, in Whose image and likeness he was made (Genesis 1:26). In man there is a spiritual and immortal soul; there is the universe in miniature, with its multiplicity and variety of form, and the marvelous order of all its parts; there is thought and will, with a vast field in which to operate; there is emotional life, with its heights and depths; there is the world of senses, with its numerous powers, perceptions, and feelings; there is the body, formed even to its minutest parts according to a teleology not yet fully grasped. Man has been made lord in this universe; freely he must direct his actions in accord with the laws of truth, goodness, and beauty, as they are manifested in nature, his social relations with his fellow men, and divine revelation.

"Since the motion picture, as has been noted, can incline the soul of the viewer to good or to evil, We will call ideal only that film which not only does not offend what We have just described, but treats it respectfully. Even that is not enough! Rather We should say: that which strengthens and uplifts man in the consciousness of his dignity, that which increases his knowledge and love of the lofty position conferred on him by his Creator; that which tells him it is possible for him to increase the gifts of energy and virtue he disposes of within himself; that which strengthens his conviction that he can overcome obstacles and avoid erroneous solutions, that he can rise after every fall and return to the right path, that he can, in sum, progress from good to better through the use of his freedom and his faculties.

"Such a motion picture would already contain the basic element of an ideal film; but more still can be attributed to it, if to respect for man is added a loving understanding of him.

Recall the touching phrase of the Lord: "I have pity on this people."

"The ideal motion picture must speak to the child in language suited to a child, to youth in a way fitted to it, to the adult as he expects to be spoken to, that is, using his own manner of seeing and understanding things," Pope Pius XII, Address to the Representatives of the Italian Movie Industry, June 21, 1955.

How far short every movie and television show falls from the ideal! This is indeed a scandal that the media which should be most helpful toward our salvation, actually lead us rapidly away from salvation toward perdition!

Let us consider Pope Pius XI's encyclical on movies:

Vigilanti Cura

Excerpts from the Encyclical letter of Pope Pius XI, July 29, 1936

In following with vigilant eye, as Our Pastoral Office requires, the beneficent work of Our Brethren in the Episcopate and of the faithful, it has been highly pleasing to Us to learn of the fruits already gathered and of the progress which continues to be made by that prudent initiative launched more than two years ago as a holy crusade against the abuses of the motion pictures and entrusted in a special manner to the "Legion of Decency".

This excellent experiment now offers Us a most welcome opportunity of manifesting more fully Our thought in regard to a matter which touches intimately the moral and religious life of the entire Christian people.

First of all, We express Our gratitude to the Hierarchy of the United States of America and to the faithful who co-operated with them, for the important results already achieved, under their direction and guidance, by the "Legion of Decency". And Our gratitude is all the livelier for the fact that We are deeply anguished to note with each passing day the lamentable progress- magni passus extra viam - of the motion picture art and industry in the portrayal of sin and vice.

As often as the occasion has presented itself, We have considered it the duty of Our high Office to direct to this condition the attention not only of the Episcopate and the Clergy but also of all men who are right-minded and solicitous for the public weal. In the Encyclical "Divini illius Magistri" We had already deplored that "potent instrumentalities of publicity (such as the cinema) which might be of great advantage to learning and education were they properly directed by healthy principles, often unfortunately serve as incentives to evil passions and are subordinated to sordid gain."

...

It is, in fact, urgently necessary to make provision that in this field also the progress of the arts, of the sciences, and of human technique and industry, since they are all true gifts of God, may be ordained to His glory and to the salvation of souls and may be made to serve in a practical way to promote the extension of the Kingdom of God upon earth. Thus, as the Church bids us pray, we may all profit by them but in such a manner as not to lose the goods eternal: "sic transeamus per bona temporalia ut non amittamus aeterna" (from the Mass of the Third Sunday after Pentecost)

Now then, it is certainty which can be readily verified that the more marvelous the progress of the motion picture art and industry, the more pernicious and deadly has it shown itself to morality and to religion and even to the very decencies of human society.

The directors of the industry in the United States recognized this fact themselves when they confessed that the responsibility before the people and the world was their own. In an agreement entered into by common accord in March, 1930, and solemnly sealed, signed, and published in the Press, they formally pledged themselves to safeguard for the future the moral welfare of the patrons of the cinema. It is promised in this agreement that no film which lowers the moral standards of the spectators, which casts discredit upon natural or human law or arouses sympathy for their violation, will be produced.

Nevertheless in spite of this wise and spontaneously taken decision, those responsible showed themselves incapable of carrying it into effect and it appeared that the producers and the operators were not disposed to stand by the principles to which they had bound themselves. Since, therefore, the above-mentioned undertaking proved to have but slight effect and since the parade of vice and crime continued on the screen, the road seemed almost closed to those who sought honest diversion in the motion picture.

Your leadership called forth the prompt and devoted loyalty of your faithful people, and millions of American Catholics signed the pledge of the "Legion of Decency" binding themselves not to attend any motion picture which was offensive to Catholic moral principles or proper standards of living.

...

Recreation, in its manifold varieties, has become a necessity for people who work under fatiguing conditions of modern industry, but it must be worthy of the rational nature of man and therefore must be morally healthy. It must be elevated to the rank of a positive factor for good and must seek to arouse noble sentiments. A people who, in time of repose, give themselves to diversion which violate decency, honor, or morality, to recreations which, especially in the young, constitute an occasion of sin, are in grave danger of losing their greatness and even their national power.

It admits of no discussion that the motion picture has achieved a position of universal importance among modern means of diversion.

...

Since then the cinema is in reality a sort of object lesson which, for good or for evil, teaches the majority of men more effectively than abstract reasoning, it must be elevated to conformity with the aims of Christian conscience and saved from depraving and demoralizing effects.

Everyone knows what damage is done to the soul by bad motion pictures (or television) They are occasions of sin; they seduce young people along the ways of evil by glorifying the passions; they show life under a false light; they cloud ideals; they destroy pure love, respect for marriage, affection for the family. They are capable also of creating prejudices among individuals and misunderstandings among nations, among social classes, among entire races.

On the other hand, good motion pictures are capable of exercising a profoundly moral influence upon those who see them. In addition to affording recreation, they are able to arouse noble ideals of life, to communicate valuable conceptions, to impart a better knowledge of the history and the beauties of the Fatherland and of other countries, to present truth and virtue under attractive forms, to create, or at least favour understanding among nations, social classes, and races, to champion the cause of justice, to give new life to the claims of virtue, and to contribute positively to the genesis of a just social order in the world.

...

It is unfortunate that, in the present state of affairs, this influence is frequently exerted for evil. So much so that when one thinks of the havoc wrought in the souls of youth and of childhood, of the loss of innocence so often suffered in the motion picture theaters, there comes to mind the terrible condemnation pronounced by Our Lord upon the corrupters of little ones: "Whosoever shall scandalize one of these little ones who believe in Me, it were better for him that a mill stone be hanged about his neck and that he be drowned in the depths of the sea."

It is therefore one of the supreme necessities of our times to watch and to labour to the end that the motion picture be no longer a school of corruption but that it be transformed into an effectual instrument for the education and the elevation of mankind.

...

It is equally the duty of the Bishops of the entire Catholic world to unite in vigilance over this universal and potent form of entertainment and instruction, to the end that they may be able to place a ban on bad motion pictures because they are an offense to the moral and religious sentiments and because they are in opposition to the Christian spirit and to its ethical principles. There must be no weariness in combating whatever contributes to the lessening of the people's sense of decency and of honor.

This is an obligation which binds not only the Bishops but also the faithful and all decent men who are solicitous for the decorum and moral health of the family, of the nation, and of human society in general.

...

Their sacred calling constrains them (the Bishops) to proclaim clearly and openly that unhealthy and impure entertainment destroys the moral fibre of a nation. They will likewise remind the motion picture industry that the demands which they make regard not only Catholics but all who patronize the cinema.

The prediction of Pope Pius XI, that unhealthy and impure entertainment destroys the moral fibre of a nation, has been fulfilled. Throughout the world all manner of vice and evil, unthinkable years ago is now common place and even receives legitimacy from various groups, including the public officials who should be protecting the common good, but are destroying all good, common or otherwise by their actions and omissions!

We are deeply anguished to note with each passing day the lamentable progress- magni passus extra viam - of the motion picture art and industry in the portrayal of sin and vices, (in 1936). This lamentable progress has now escalated to new heights of sin and vice which were probably unimaginable in Pope Pius XI's day!

Since, therefore, the above-mentioned undertaking proved to have but slight effect and since the parade of vice and crime continued on the screen, the road seemed almost closed to those who sought honest diversion in the motion picture. The road, which was almost closed in 1936, is certainly virtually impassable today with the increase in depravity in movies and television! Pope Pius XI reminds us that all of us have a duty in this regard, not just the clergy. Let us make the

Pledge of the Legion of Decency our own, since it is based on the Natural Law, which is written on our hearts.

The responsibility of those people who make the radio an instrument of intellectual or moral corruption presents no problem; it merely calls for the brand of infamy. That of the indifferent, the apathetic, the skeptical, very great reason of the serious and often imperceptible consequences, calls for something else; it confronts us with the difficulty-a difficulty rather than a problem of making him understand that he is doing wrong.

The problem arises when it is a question of presenting, with honest and often praiseworthy intentions, arguments, events, or questions legitimately interesting and useful from a literary, artistic, psychological, moral or social point of view. And this is what then perplexes the mind: Should we hold our peace when it might be fitting of necessary to speak, or should we speak and run the risk of alarming certain ears, perturbing certain souls, but above all of contaminating the candid innocence of childish hearts? Adults have only themselves to blame, for their indiscreet or unwise curiosity; but what about the children who, thoughtlessly and without serious malice, so easily evade on this point their parent's supervision? It is the duty of a speaker over the radio to use a language of such tact and reticence that he may be understood by adults without rousing the imagination or troubling the simplicity of the young., Pope Pius XII Address to Radio Announcers, April 22, 1948.

The Fathers on the Theater

St. John Chrysostom in his Baptismal Instruction states:

"Let there be no more talk about the hippodrome and the lawless spectacle of the theatre, for they provide the fuel for licentiousness; let there be no talk of the cruel pleasure derived from the combat of wild beasts and men. For what pleasure is there in watching a fellow human, who shares in the same nature as yourself, being mangled by savage beasts? Are you not afraid, do you not shudder, for fear that a thunderbolt might fall from on high and set your head ablaze? For it is you, one might say, who sharpen the teeth of the beast. You, by your shouts have a personal part in the murder, if not by your hand, at least by your tongue."

St. Augustine in his First Catechetical Instruction reminds us:

"There are also men who neither seek to be rich nor go about striving the vain pomp of honor, but wish to find their pleasure and satisfaction in gluttony (and drunkenness) and debaucheries (i.e. lust), in theatres and frivolous shows, which they have free of charge in great cities. (which can be found on television now) But thus they also both squander their small means in riotous living, and afterwards under pressure of want, breakout into thefts and burglaries, and sometimes even into highway robberies, and are suddenly filled with fears both numerous and great, and they who a little before were singing in the tavern now dream of the sorrows of prison. Moreover, in their eager pursuit of the games, they become like demons as they incite men by their cries to kill one another and to engage in furious contests, men who have done no injury to one another, but desire only to please a frantic mob; and if they observe that they are peaceably disposed, they straightway hate and persecute them, and raise a cry for them to be clubbed, on the ground that they are in collusion; and in this wickedness they compel even the judge who is the avenger of wickedness to commit. But if they perceive that they wreak their most frightful enmity upon each other-whether they be what are called 'sintae' or actors and the stage-chorus, or charioteer, or common gladiators, poor wretches whom they pit in a fighting contest against one another, not only men against men, but even men against wild beasts-and the fiecer the fury with which they perceive them to rage against one another, the more they love them and delight in them. They second them when in fury, and rouse it by seconding them, the spectators themselves being madder against each other, as they second this combatant or that, than those whose madness they madly provoke, and whom they madly, too, desire to gaze upon. How, then, can the mind which feeds on dissension and strife perserve the health which comes from peace? For as the food taken, so is the resulting state of health. Finally, though mad pleausres are no pleasures, yet of whatever kind they are, and however much the display of riches, the pride of honors, and the the devouring gluttony of taverns, and the factions of the theatres, and the uncleanness of fornication, and the lasciviousness of the baths give delight, yet one little fever carries all these things away, and robs them of the whole vain happiness of their life while yet alive. There remains a void and wounded conscience which shall experience the judgement of God whose protection it disdained to have; and shall find in Him a severe Lord whom it scorned to seek and love as a gentle Father."

What would St. Augustine say today, when the theater is brought into the home and rather than being watched for a couple of hours in the evening runs morning, noon and night? What would St. Augustine say about a boxing match, "whom they pit in a fighting contest against one another"? Think well how much time is squandered before the television, and then consider what St. Augustine says next:

"But you, inasmuch as you are seeking that true rest which is promised to Christians after this life, shall taste its sweetness and comfort even here amid the bitterest afflictions of this life, if you love the commandments of Him who has promised it. For quickly will you realize that the fruits of goodness are sweeter than those of iniquity, and that a man finds a more genuine and pleasurable joy in a good conscience amidst afflictions than he who has a bad conscience amid delights; for you have not come to be joined to the Church of God with the object of seeking some temporal advantage."

"Seated where there is nothing of God, will one be thinking of his Maker?" Absolutely not. Even if there were no other objection, this one would be sufficient reason to consider turning away.

Saint Alphonsus says:

"And let it be remembered that females who keep their breast uncovered, or dress immodestly in any other way, are guilty of the sin of scandal, as also actors in immodest comedies, and still more the persons who compose such comedies; also painters who paint obscene pictures, and the heads of families who keep such pictures in their houses." [31]

"A parent should forbid his children to wear masks, to go to dances, or to act a part in comedies." [32]

"Be careful also not to permit your sons to act a part in comedies, nor even to be present at an immodest comedy. A young man or woman goes to such comedies in the grace of God, and returns home his enemy. Do not allow your children to go to certain festivities (which are feasts of the devil) in which there is dancing, courtships, immodest singing, and sinful amusements. "Where there is dancing," says St. Ephrem, "there a feast of the devil is celebrated." But you will say, "We only jest; what harm is there in that?" "They are not amusements," says St. Peter Chrysologus, "but greivous offenses against God."" [33]

"The unhappy soul will then say: Had I mortified myself by not looking at such an object; ... if I had read a spiritual book every day;" [34]

---

[31]   Golden Book of the Commandments and Sacraments, page 33
[32]   Ibid page 67
[33]   Ibid page 85
[34]   Preparation for Death page 285

"... he who is ... wholly absorbed with the attractions of the theatre and ballroom can have no valid claim to the title of faithful Catholic." [35]

"Beware of trying to find out the faults of your neighbor." [36]

"If in your presence unbecoming and sinful language is used, leave the company if it is possible to do so." [37]

Let us consider that is anything evil comes on television, there is a button on it to end the evil and turn it off. Then we should say a prayer askign God's forgiveness for all involved and that He may enlighten them to the millions of sins they participating in by scandal.

The Breviary comments on Saint Peter Chrysologus:

"The people had a custom of assisting on the first day of January at certain games, which consisted of theatrical performances and dances; the saint repressed these by the severity with which he preached against them. One of his expressions deserves to be handed down: 'He that jests with the devil, can never enjoy the company of Christ.'"

A story from the Cure of Ars

St. Augustine gives us a good example of this. He tells us that he once had a friend, a young man, who led a perfectly good life.

One day he was in the company of his fellow-students, who did not like it that he always lived and acted differently from them. They urged him to go with them to the amphitheater, where there was a prize-fight among men. As our young friend detested such shows, he resisted with all his might. Finally they urged him so much, that he consented with the words:

"Very well. I will go with you, but only my body will be there standing among you. My mind and my eyes will not partake in this horrible spectacle."

---

[35]   12 Steps to Holiness and Salvation page 16
[36]   Ibid page 63
[37]   Ibid page 161

So they led him forth, and, while the whole multitude went wild with barbarous delight, the young man took no part and kept his eyes shut. Would that he had also stopped his ears, for at a certain great noise curiosity got the better of him and he opened his eyes. That was sufficient to ruin him. The more he saw the more delighted was he, and after that there was no need of urging him to visit the place. He was only too eager to go there and to induce others to go with him.

"Oh, my Lord!" exclaimed St. Augustine, "who will lead him away from this abyss? The grace of God alone can do it!"

From <u>De Spectaculis</u>

Tertullian
From 'De Spectaculis'
Chapter 27 begins with something that is common in movies and on television of all kinds: "We ought to detest these heathen meetings and assemblies, if on no other account than that there God's Name is blasphemed." This is objectively a mortal sin and should not be said or listened to!

"Ye Servants of God, about to draw near to God, that you may make solemn consecration of yourselves to Him, seek well to understand the condition of faith, the reasons of the Truth, the laws of Christian discipline, which forbid among other sins of the world, the pleasures of public shows." (Note this would apply to movies, sporting events and television.)

"For such is the power of earthly pleasures, that, to retain the opportunity of still partaking of them, it contrives to prolong a willing ignorance, and bribes knowledge into playing a dishonest part."

"It, therefore, it shall be made plain that the entire apparatus of shows is based upon idolatry, beyond all doubt that will carry with it the conclusion that our renunciatory testimony in the laver of baptism has reference to the shows, which through their idolatry, have been given over to the devil, and his pomp, and his angels." The modern doctrine of Do what thou wilt, which came out in the 1960's as Do your own thing, is promulgated and promoted in movies and on television, as well as all manner of perversity.

"If, then, we keep throat and belly free from such defilements, how much more do we withhold our nobler parts, our ears and eyes, from the idolatrous and funereal enjoyments, which are not passed through the body, but are digested in the very spirit and soul, whose purity, much more than that of our bodily organs, God as a right to claim from us."

"But is we ought to abominate all that is immodest, on what ground is it right to hear what we must not speak? ... What you reject in deed, you are not to bid welcome in word."

"For the show always leads to spiritual agitation, since where there is pleasure, there is keenness of feeling giving pleasure its zest; and there there is keenness of feeling, there is rivalry giving in turn its zest."

Frequenting Theaters.

From <u>Theory and Practice of the Confessional</u>

"Theatrical performances (in the wider sense of the term) are, according to the teaching of St. Thomas, [38] secundum se, not sinful, but may become gravely so, by offending against religion and good morals, in the matter represented or in the manner of representing it. Very many modern dramas are of the latter kind, and full of dangers, treating as they do of anti-religious subjects or of such as are hostile to faith, or lascivious; degrading the Catholic faith, distorting historical facts to its detriment, extolling the enemies of the Church, holding up holy rites and even the Sacraments of the Church to mockery and contempt, calumniating priests, making vices, such as adultery, revenge, suicide, and sins of the flesh, appear lawful or even glorifying them; characterizing religion in general as ridiculous, superstitious, etc., treating not only of obscene and dangerous subjects, but also offending decency in the manner of representation.

"If, therefore, the dramas in question are notably contrary to religion (Religioni notabiliter contraria), or if the subject-matter or the manner of representing it are nimis turpia (too base), attendance is certainly a grave sin. For what may not be seen, or heard, or read, extra

---

[38] II. II Q. 168, art. 3. 431 S. Thorn. 4 Sent. dist. 16, Q. 4, art 2.

theatrum, without great sin, cannot be, as the Angelic Master expresses himself, ratione theatri leviora. (the lighter aspect of the theater)

"If they are notably, but not nimis turpia, (very bad) they may be occasio relativa, (a relative occasion of sin) and frequenting them out of curiosity or for amusement (if there is no danger of consenting in turpem delectationem (against the sixth commandment)) may be free from grave sin. But this danger will, in the case of young people, be absent only when they have very tender consciences, conduct themselves very prudently, and when, after being repeatedly present at such performances, they are able to say that they have not committed mortal sin. Performances, however, which are non notabiliter turpia (is not notably base), may be an occasio proximo, for those who know by experience their own weakness, the more so as nowadays doubtful attractions are introduced even into otherwise good or harmless plays.

"The so-called choreas scenicae (ballet), quae inter actus miscentur, utpote in quibus ob vestitum saltatricum, obscaenos saltandi modos aut lascivas gesticulationes, maxima apparere solet turpitudo, will probably be for many theatergoers an occasio proxima. (stage-dancing, which act between the mix with men, whom for their clothing as being in a dancing, wanton, or modes of dance-visaged debauchees gestures, eg, the greatest turpitude is wont to appear.)

When, therefore, one goes to a theater without exercising any discrimination as to the choice of the play or the manner of its performance, he exposes himself to a probable danger of sin, ex communiter contingentibus fit prudens praesumptio. Some, however, maintain that they attend chiefly to the music, not to the plot and its representation; this, of course, would materially reduce the danger, but not wholly remove it.

"Frequenting the theater may also become sinful on account of the sinful intention connected with it, and by the scandal thereby given. Besides the actors and actresses in a bad play, those also give scandal who cooperate in spectacula notabiliter turpia (notably base spectacles or gravely adverse to religion) aut Religioni graviter adversa, positively, by money or applause, and, negatively, by not preventing them when ex officio they were bound to do so, or at least could have prevented them by some other means; for example, by refusing to cooperate, etc. [39] Moreover, parents and other superiors give scandal

---

[39] Cf. S. Alph. Lib. III. n. 427. 433 Ibid.

who do not effectually prevent their children and those under their care from being present at improper representations, or when they give permission to go there, without having previously ascertained the character of the play. Finally, those give scandal who encourage others (especially young people) by their example to attend theaters, also clerics and religious who, contrary to ecclesiastical regulations, are present at secular performances. [40]

"If, therefore, by going to the theater, a person exposes himself to only slight danger, and only gives slight scandal, he is free from grave sin if he takes the necessary precautions.

"But if he suffers great danger, or gives great scandal, only a causa gravis (grave cause) would excuse him from grave sin if he takes the necessary precautions, and tries to the best of his power to make good the scandal. Such causa gravis would be, for instance, a well-founded fear of great detriment, continued irritation of parents, of husband or wife, etc.; the loss of the subscription fee would not be a causa sufficiens. But even when there is a causa, and, in spite of precautions, faith is endangered, or if the person often succumbs to temptation, he is absolutely bound to avoid the occasion. Hence no causa will excuse frequentation of a very immoral or godless performance, because it will not be possible to avoid the formal danger which accompanies it.

"In cases where it is necessary, the penitent must be strictly bound to avoid the theater or certain plays; even where this obligation is not strictly binding, he must still be persuaded to avoid the theater, and if this is not possible or opportune, the priest must at least instruct the penitent cautiously to conduct himself.

"The actors in immoral and godless plays cannot, of course, be admitted to the Sacraments till they have either given up their profession, or no longer take part in such performances, for they are peccatores publici, publicum scandalum prabentes. (public sinners) [41]

---

[40] Benedict XIV, De Synod. Lib. II. cp. 10, n. 11. Cf. S. Alph. Lib. III.
[41] Cf. Aertnys, 1. c. n. 327; Lehmkuhl, 1. c. P. I. L. II. cp. 3, n. 644.

The Church on Books and Reading

Much has been said on this subject. By analogy we can apply the same principles to television, movies and the theater that we apply to books.

By the law itself are forbidden (by Canon 1399):

1. Editions of the original text or of ancient Catholic versions of the Sacred Scriptures (including those of the Oriental Church), published by any non-Catholics whatsoever; likewise translations of these texts made or published by non-Catholics;

2. books of any writers defending heresy or schism, or tending in any way to undermine the very foundations of religion;

3. books which avowedly attack religion or good morals;

4. books of any non-Catholics treating professedly of religion, unless it is certain that they contain nothing contrary to the Catholic faith;

5. books of Sacred Scripture, note and commentaries thereon, and translations which have been published without the permission required by Canon 1385 and Canon 1391; books and pamphlets which give an account of new apparitions, revelations, visions, prophecies, or miracles, or which introduce new devotions (even if it is claimed that the devotions are private), unless the precepts of the Canons regarding their publication have been observed;

6. books which attack or ridicule any of the Catholic dogmas, or which defend errors condemned by the Holy See, or which disparage divine worship, or strive to overthrow ecclesiastical discipline, or which have the avowed aim of defaming the ecclesiastical hierarchy or the clerical or religious states;

7. books which teach or approve of any kind of superstition, fortune-telling, divination, magic, communication with spirits, and other things of that kind;

8. books which declare duels, suicide, or divorce as licit; which treat of the masonic and other similar sects, and contend that these are not pernicious, but rather useful to the Church and civil society;

9. books which professedly discuss, describe or teach impure or obscene topics;

10. editions of liturgical books approved by the Holy See, which have been unlawfully changed in some particulars so that they no longer agree with the authentic and approved editions.

11. books which publish indulgences which are apocryphal, or which are condemned or recalled by the Holy see;

12. any images whatsoever of Our Lord, of the Blessed Virgin, of the angels, or of the saints or other servants of God, which are not in harmony with the spirit and Decrees of the Church.

It should be noted that on October 14, 1966, Paul VI removed this Canon from the Code of Canon Law, thus in effect permitting pornography.

Before proceeding to the relation of Canon 1399 to radio, television and movies, we shall consider the necessary permission to read forbidden books and the precautions involved:

"Cardinals and bishops (both residential and titular) and other Ordinaries, are not bound by the ecclesiastical prohibition of books provided they employ the necessary precautions," Canon 1401

Although these men are supposed to be quite learned in theological matters and able to investigate forbidden matters and must do so in the discharge of their office on occasion, they are reminded that this necessary occasion of sin, coming from their office, requires them to take precautions to avoid sin. These books condemned by Canon 1399 ipso facto, by their very existence are dangerous and if the most learned and holy members of the Church (as Bishops and Cardinals should be) are warned to take precautions, how much more dangerous are these books to other clerics and laymen, who are less learned in these matters?

"In the case of books forbidden by the general law of the Church or by Decree of the Holy See, Ordinaries can give their subject permission to read only individual books and in urgent cases only. If the Ordinaries have obtained from the Holy See a general faculty to allow their subjects to keep and read forbidden books, they shall grant this permission only with discretion and for a good and reasonable cause." Canon 1402.

"The permission to read forbidden books exempts nobody from the prohibition of the natural law, which forbids the reading of books which are for the particular reader a proximate occasion of sin. Local Ordinaries and others who have the care of souls shall on opportune occasions warn the faithful of the danger and harm of reading bad books, especially such as have been forbidden." Canon 1405

Although a person has obtained permission to read condemned books for some reason, he may not do so, if they are a proximate occasion of sin. In this case the provisions of the natural law override the permission obtained under ecclesiastical law. Therefore the general principle is that any work, which is a proximate occasion of sin must be avoided, no matter what source it comes from. (ie. books, radio, television, etc.)

An excommunication reserved to the Apostolic See in a special manner is incurred ipso facto by the publishers of books written by apostates, heretics and schismatics in defense of apostasy, heresy or schism; also by persons who defend or knowingly read or retain (in their possession) without due permission the above mentioned books and others which have been by name forbidden by Apostolic Letters., Canon 2318, paragraph 1

It should be obvious that we cannot claim to be followers of Blessed Jesus, if we contradict the ethical principles of the Gospel and refuse to follow the command, "If any man will come after Me," said

He, "let him deny himself and take up his cross, and follow Me." (Matthew 26:24)

"And we find some writers who have gone to such lengths of boldness and impudence as to propagate in their books those very vices which the Apostle forbade to be so much as mentioned by Christians. "But fornication, and all uncleanness ... let it not so much as named among you, as becometh saints." (Ephesians 5:3). Oh that such men might learn at last that they cannot serve two masters, God and lust, religion and impurity! "He that is not with Me is against Me.", said the Lord Jesus (Matthew 12:30), and certainly those writers are not with Christ, who by their filthy descriptions poison morality, which is the true basis of civil and domestic society. In consideration, therefore, of the deluge of filthy literature which is pouring in a rising flood upon practically all nations, this Supreme Sacred Congregation of the Holy Office, which is intrusted with the guardianship of faith and morals, does by apostolic authority and in the name of His Holiness, by Divine Providence Pope Pius XI, command all Ordinaries of places to strive by all means in their power to remedy so great and so urgent an evil. Certainly it is the part of those who have been placed by the Holy Ghost to rule the Church of God to exercise an alert and diligent watchfulness over everything that is printed and published in their dioceses. Everyone knows that books which nowadays are current all over the world are too numerous to be examined by the Holy See. Hence, Pius X of happy memory declared in his Motu Proprio, 'Sacrorum Antistitum': "Whatever books are current in your dioceses of such a nature as to be harmful to readers, make earnest efforts to get rid of them, even by solemn proscription. For although the Holy See is making every effort to get rid of such books, they have already grown so numerous that it is scarcely possible to examine them all. And so the remedy often comes too late, after the evil through long delay has grown inveterate."

"And yet the greater part of those volumes and booklets, although most pernicious, cannot be condemned by a special censure of this Supreme Congregation. hence, the Ordinaries, according to Canon 1397, paragraph 4, must, either by themselves or through the Council of Vigilance which the same Supreme Pontiff established by his Encyclical, 'Pascendi dominici gregis', constantly and earnestly strive to fulfill this most important duty; and they should not fail to denounce those books, as occasion offers, in their diocesan papers, as condemned and extremely harmful.

"Moreover, as everyone knows, the Church has already provided by general law that all books which are tainted with immorality, and which of set purpose or openly attack the integrity of morals, be regarded as forbidden just as if they had actually been placed on the Index of forbidden books. It follows that persons who without due permission read a book that is undoubtedly salacious, even though it is not condemned by name by the ecclesiastical authorities, commit a mortal sin. And since in this most important matter false and disastrous opinions are current among the faithful, Ordinaries of places must see to it that especially pastors and their assistants give attention to this matter and give the needed instruction to the people.

"Besides, the Ordinaries must not fail to declare openly according to the needs of their respective dioceses, what books by name are forbidden by the law itself. and if they think that they can more effectively or speedily protect the faithful from any particular book by condemning it by special decree, they must by all means make use of this power, just as the Holy see commonly does when grave reasons require it, according to Canon 1395, paragraph 1: "The right and duty of forbidding books for grave cause belongs not only to the supreme ecclesiastical authority for the universal Church, but also to particular Councils and Ordinaries of places, for their subjects."

"Finally, this Supreme Sacred Congregation orders all Archbishops, Bishops and other Ordinaries of places, on the occasion of their diocesan report, to make known to the Holy See what measures they have taken and put into execution against lascivious books., Holy Office, Instruction, 3 May, 1927.

Although directed mainly to Ordinaries, there are things in this instruction that apply equally to all. Ordinaries were told to get rid of objectionable books, because the volume of them is so great that the Apostolic See is no longer able to keep up. If this is true in 1927, when the Curia was a massive operation, how much more so today, when the Apostolic See consists of the Pope assisted by a few Catholic laymen! We remind the faithful of their duty to denounce evil books, movies, television to the proper ecclesiastical authorities. (i.e. their Ordinary)

It follows that persons who without due permission read a book that is undoubtedly salacious, even though it is not condemned by name by the ecclesiastical authorities, commit a mortal sin.

On the occasion of condemning and placing on the Index all the works of one Albert Pincherle (or Moravia), the Holy Office proceeded to say: "On this occasion the Most Emminent and Most Reverend Fathers, deploring the immense harm that is done to souls, first by the unrestrained license to publish and diffuse books, booklets, and periodicals (and other forms of communication, such as radio, television and movies) which of set purpose narrate, describe, and teach things that are lacivious and obscene, and also by the fatal eagerness to read such matter indiscriminately, decided to issue the following warnings:

"To all the faithful: that they remember their very grave obligation to abstain entirely from the reading of such books and periodicals; To those who have charge of the instruction and education of youth: that, conscious of their grave responsibility, they keep their charges away from such writings entirely, as from an insidious poison;

"Finally, to those who in virtue of their office have the responsibility of regulating the morality of citizens: that they do not permit such writings, which strive to subvert the very principles and foundations of natural morality, to be published and distributed. On the 3rd day of April, 1952, in the audience granted as usual to His Excellency the Most Reverend Assessor of the Holy Office, His Holiness Pope Pius XII approved the resolution of the Eminent Fathers when it was reported to him, confirmed it and ordered that it be published."

Given at Rome, from the Holy Office, 20 May, 1952.

An Instruction of the Holy Office to Archbishops, Bishops, and other Ordinaries of places on sensual and sensual-mystic literature, is as follows:

"Among the most terrible of the evils which in our age are utterly undermining the moral teaching of Christ, and doing so much harm to souls redeemed by His precious Blood, a prominent place belongs to that type of literature which exploits sensuality and lust, or even a certain lascivious mysticism. To this class belongs especially certain romances, fanciful tales, plays, and comedies - types of literature of which our age is remarkably prolific, and which are daily being produced in increasing quantities.

"Such works of literary art, which exert so great an influence upon many persons, especially among young people, if only they kept within the bounds of decency, which certainly are not too narrow, would be able not only to afford innocent pleasure, but even to elevate the morals of the reader.

"But the fact is, alas, that this abundance of books which combine a frivolous fascination with immorality, is the cause of a very great loss of souls. For many of these writers depict immodesties in flaming imagery; relate the most obscene details, sometimes guardedly, sometimes openly and shamelessly, without the least regard for the requirements of modesty; they describe even the worst carnal vices with subtle analysis, and adorn them will all the brilliancy and allurements of style, to such a degree that nothing in the field of morals is left inviolate. It is easy to see haw harmful all this is, especially to young people, in whom the fire of youth makes chastity more difficult. These books, often small in size, are sold at low prices in book stores, on the streets and squares of cities, at railroad stations; they come very quickly into everybody's hands, and bring great and often fateful dangers to Catholic families. For it is well known that writing of that sort violently excites the imagination, wildly inflames the passions, and drags the heart into the mire of impurity.

"There is a kind of love story worse than the rest, being written by authors who, to their shame, do not hesitate to give their sensuality the appearance of rectitude by blending it with sacred things. Into their stories of impure love they weave a sort of piety toward God and a very false religious mysticism; as if faith could be consistent with the neglect, or rather the impudent denial of a right moral standard; or the virtue of religion be found associated with immorality! On the contrary the teaching of the Church is that no one can attain eternal life, no matter how firmly he may believe the truths of revelation, unless <u>he keeps the commandments of God</u>; for one who professes faith in Christ and does not follow the footsteps of Christ is not deserving even of the name Christian. "Faith without works is dead" (James 2:6). And our Saviour warns us: "Not everyone that saith to Me, Lord, Lord, shall enter into the Kingdom of Heaven: but he that doth the will of My Father who is in heaven, he shall enter into the Kingdom of Heaven.

"Let no one make these excuses; that many of those books have a truly admirable brilliance and elegance of style; that they are remarkable for inculcating a psychology in accord with modern discoveries; that the lascivious bodily pleasures are reprobated in as much as they are represented in their true light as most foul, or are sometimes shown to be connected with qualms of conscience, or in as much as it is shown how often the basest pleasures give way at last to the sorrow of a sort of repentance. For neither elegance of style not medical or philosophic lore-if indeed these are things to be found in that sort of writing-nor the intention of the authors, whatever it may be, can prevent the readers, who owing to the corruption of nature are usually very weak and must inclined to impurity, from being gradually enmeshed in the allurements of those unclean pages, from becoming depraved in mind and heart, and finally from throwing away the reins that curb their passions, falling into all kinds of sins, and at times, grown weary of a life full of squalor, even committing suicide.

"It is not to be wondered at that the world, which seeks its own even to the contempt of God, should be delighted with such books and should spread them; but it is very deplorable that writers who call themselves Christian should give their time and talent to such deadly literature. can one who contradicts the ethical principles of the Gospel, yet be a follower of the Blessed Jesus who commanded all men to crucify their flesh with its vices and concupiscences? "If any man will come after Me," said He, "let him deny himself and take up his cross, and follow Me." (Matthew 26:24)

"And we find some writers who have gone to such lengths of boldness and impudence as to propagate in their books those very vices which the Apostle forbade to be so much as mentioned by Christians. "But fornication, and all uncleanness ... let it not so much as named among you, as becometh saints." (Ephesians 5:3). Oh that such men might learn at last that they cannot serve two masters, God and lust, religion and impurity! "He that is not with Me is against Me.", said the Lord Jesus (Matthew 12:30), and certainly those writers are not with Christ, who by their filthy descriptions poison morality, which is the true basis of civil and domestic society.

"In consideration, therefore, of the deluge of filthy literature which is pouring in a rising flood upon practically all nations, this Supreme Sacred Congregation of the Holy Office, which is intrusted with the guardianship of faith and morals, does by apostolic authority and in the name of His Holiness, by Divine Providence Pope Pius XI, command all Ordinaries of places to strive by all means in their power to remedy so great and so urgent an evil.

"Certainly it is the part of those who have been placed by the Holy Ghost to rule the Church of God to exercise an alert and diligent watchfulness over everything that is printed and published in their dioceses. Everyone knows that books which nowadays are current all over the world are too numerous to be examined by the Holy See. Hence, Pius X of happy memory declared in his Motu Proprio, 'Sacrorum Antistitum': "Whatever books are current in your dioceses of such a nature as to be harmful to readers, make earnest efforts to get rid of them, even by solemn proscription. For although the Holy See is making every effort to get rid of such books, they have already grown so numerous that it is scarcely possible to examine them all. And so the remedy often comes too late, after the evil through long delay has grown inveterate."

"And yet the greater part of those volumes and booklets, although most pernicious, cannot be condemned by a special censure of this Supreme Congregation. hence, the Ordinaries, according to Canon 1397, paragraph 4, must, either by themselves or through the Council of Vigilance which the same Supreme Pontiff established by his Encyclical, Pascendi dominici gregis, constantly and earnestly strive to fulfill this most important duty; and they should not fail to denounce those books, as occasion offers, in their diocesan papers, as condemned and extremely harmful.

"Moreover, as everyone knows, the Church has already provided by general law that all books which are tainted with immorality, and which of set purpose or openly attack the integrity of morals, be regarded as forbidden just as if they had actually been placed on the Index of forbidden books. it follows that persons who without due permission read a book that is undoubtedly salacious, even though it is not condemned by name by the ecclesiastical authorities, commit a mortal sin. And since in this most important matter false and disastrous opinions are current among the faithful, Ordinaries of places must see to it that especially pastors and their assistants give attention to this matter and give the needed instruction to the people.

"Besides, the Ordinaries must not fail to declare openly according to the needs of their respective dioceses, what books by name areforbidden by the law itself. and if they think that they can more effectively or speedily protect the faithful from any particular book by condemning it by special decree, they must by all means make use of this power, just as the

Holy see commonly does when grave reasons require it, according to Canon 1395, paragraph 1: "The right and duty of forbidding books for grave cause belongs not only to the supreme ecclesiastical authority for the universal Church, but also to particular Councils and Ordinaries of places, for their subjects." Finally, this Supreme Sacred Congregation orders all Archbishops, Bishops and other Ordinaries of places, on the occasion of their diocesan report, to make known to the Holy See what measures they have taken and put into execution against lascivious books. Holy Office, Instruction, 3 May, 1927.

Some of these warnings may be repetitious, but how many have repeatedly watched reruns of immoral television programs with giving it any thought. Better to repeat a warning, than to find that one has not been properly warned.

In his Encyclical, Immortale Dei of November 1, 1885, Pope Leo XIII states:

"So, too, the liberty of thinking, and of publishing, whatsoever one likes, without any hindrance, is not in itself an advantage over which society can wisely rejoice. On the contrary, it is the fountain-head and origin of many evils. Liberty is a power perfecting man, and hence should have truth and goodness for its object. But the character of goodness and truth cannot be changed at option. These remain ever one and the same, and are no less changeable than nature herself. If the mind assents to false opinions, and the will chooses and follows after what is wrong, neither can attain its native fullness, but both must fall from their native dignity into an abyss of corruption. Whatever, therefore, is opposed to virtue and truth, may not rightly be brought temptingly before the eye of man, must less sanctioned by the favour and protection of law. A well-spent life is the only passport to heaven, whither all are bound, and on this account the State is acting against the laws and dictates of nature whenever it permits license of opinion and of action to lead minds astray from truth, and souls away from the practice of virtue.

"On the question of the separation of the Church and State the same Pontiff (Gregory XVI) writes as follows: "Nor can we hope for happier results, either for religion or for the civil government, from the wishes of those who desire that the Church be separated from the State, and the concord between the secular and ecclesiastical authority be dissolved. It is clear that these men, who yearn for a shameless liberty, live in dread of an agreement which has always been fraught with good, and advantageous alike to sacred and civil interests."

"So, too, the liberty of thinking, and of publishing, whatsoever one likes, without any hindrance, is not in itself an advantage over which society can wisely rejoice. On the contrary, it is the fountain-head and origin of many evils." This principle must always be in our minds. The license to do as one pleases, which is taught by Satanism (do what thou wilt) and his diabolical system is the road to hell. Since one may not publish or broadcast evil, one may not partake of it, when another publishes or broadcasts it. We are not free in this matter to follow our own will, but must conform to the Divine and Natural Laws, as well as to the prudent provisions of Ecclesiastical Law."

In the Encyclical, <u>Libertas Humana</u>, of June 20, 1888, Pope Leo XIII writes:

"We must now consider briefly liberty of speech, and liberty of the press. It is hardly necessary to say that there can be no such right as this, if it be not used in moderation, and if it pass beyond the bounds and ends of all true liberty. For right is a moral power which-as We have before said and must again and again repeat-it is absurd to suppose that nature has accorded indifferently to truth and falsehood, to justice and injustice. Men have a right freely and prudently to propagate throughout the State what things soever are true and honorable, so that as many as possible may possess them; but lying opinions, than which no mental plague is greater, and vices which corrupt the heart and moral life should be diligently repressed by public authority, lest they insidiously work the ruin of the State. The excesses of an unbridled intellect, which unfailingly end in the oppression of the untutored multitude, are no less rightly controlled by the authority of the law than are the injuries inflicted by violence upon the weak. And this all the more surely, because by far the greater part of the community is either absolutely unable, or able only with great difficulty, to escape from illusions and deceitful subtleties, especially such as flatter the passions. If unbridled license of speech and of writing be granted to all, nothing will remain sacred and inviolate; even the highest and truest mandates of nature, justly held to be the common and noblest heritage of the human race, will not be spared. Thus, truth being gradually obscured by darkness, pernicious and manifold error, as too often happens, will easily prevail. Thus, too, license will fein what liberty loses; for liberty will ever be more free and secure, in proportion as license is kept in fuller restraint. In regard, however, to any matters of opinion which God leaves to man's free discussion, full liberty of thought and speech is naturally within the right of every one; for such liberty never leads men to suppress truth, but often to discover it and make it known."

"But lying opinions, than which no mental plague is greater, and vices which corrupt the heart and moral life, should be diligently repressed by public authority lest they insidiously work the ruin of the State." Since the State has decided it wishes ruin and has refused to suppress the evil spewing forth on the air waves and in print, each member of the faithful must avoid lying opinions and vices which corrupt the heart, lest they come to personal ruin.

From <u>Divine Contemplation For All</u>

pages 104-6

On the other hand, the world, too, imposes a mighty deal of reading on its votaries: Periodicals without number-filled with deliberate lies, or suppressions of the truth, to suit the needs of political parties; with unwholesome, poisonous, vitriolic, hellish faits divers; faked history; with garbage literature of infinite variety, pandering to all the morbid appetites of an effete society and books of demi-science, with trumpery articles on all the branches of human speculation, creating the impression that man, puny man, has solved all the riddles of the universe, fathomed all the great deeps above his head and under his feet, and weighed God in the balance and found Him wanting! man, that thing of yesterday, whose body, to-morrow, rots in the grave, while his soul goes to its judgment!

From such mental seed what harvest can be expected but utter bewilderment, anarchy of thought, desperate materialism with its attendant evils? -A plentiful crop of these evils we see ripening under our eyes, promising a terrible reaping in the near future. The horrible world war (i) we have just gone through; the present labour unrest with its arrogant, unreasonable demands; Bolshevism rampant everywhere: what are these but the fruits of that precious so-called liberty of the Press? This is not liberty, but most unbridled license- license to utter, declaim, print, read, disseminate broadcast, without check or restraint, monstrous, immoral, blasphemous, subversive doctrines. A stronger social order than ours would soon suffer disintegration under such powerful dissolvents. As for the effect on the individual-it is simply frightful.

Do most people in our midst, now-a-days, know whether there is a God? or whether they have an immortal soul? or whether there is such a thing as moral responsibility? They are no longer quite sure of anything. They hold that it would be wrong for anyone to rob them or kill them: but it is not so clear to them that, for instance, adultery is a crime. One thing only looms big before their mental vision: they must have what they call "a good time"; they want to amuse themselves-and following out this simple programme, they proceed to make a hash of their lives. And under all their dissipation, there is a sadness bordering upon despair.

If a Christian dabbles in this sort of literature, he unfits himself for divine contemplation. If he must touch it, through no choice of his own, and under pressure of circumstances, he must surround himself with every sanitary precaution that prudence can suggest, otherwise he runs a mortal risk: he is like a man who would rashly handle poisonous gases, or powerful acids, without putting on a mask to protect his face, or gloves to save his hands.

There are those among the educated and wealthy who think that they cannot possibly find a place in the order of their day for holy reading. Let me tell them bluntly: You do not want to; you have no relish for it. That is the plain truth.

No time for holy reading! If those same unworthy Christians would write down an enumeration of all the items of newspapers, novels, and other frivolous reading they contrive to get into a week, they would be amazed at the quantity. Now it is simply a case of, Ceci tuera cela: this will kill that. Either holy reading or pernicious reading: it is clear that the two cannot thrive together: either holy reading and as its fruit, divine contemplation; or no holy reading at all, and, as a fatal consequence, no divine contemplation at all.

Bishop Hedley on Reading

From <u>A Bishop and His Flock</u>, 1903

Books and newspapers may be occasions of sin; immoral books; sensuous books; idle reading Precautions with regards to newspapers and books destructive of faith. Good books tend to give an adequate knowledge of our holy religion, and to instruct us in the spiritual life.

The printing press is one of the greatest of the forces of the modern world. Books and newspapers are not only beyond all counting, but they are absolute necessaries of life, even to the poorest; and they work more good and more mischief than armies and parliaments. It will not, therefore, be inopportune to say a few words about READING.

There are those who read too much, or with too little discretion and self-restraint; and there are those who neglect to read what they ought. Let us first speak of want of discretion in reading.

It stands to reason that if a book or a newspaper is an occasion of sin, it has to be given up or let alone. All Catholics are taught and no other doctrine can be reconciled with the Gospel of Jesus Christ that if a thing is sinful to do, it is sinful to expose oneself unnecessarily to a temptation to do it, and sinful to dwell upon it in the heart, with desire, or even with any kind of lingering consideration. This is especially true of all that regards anger, hatred, or impurity. With respect to theft, violence, murder, or impiety, it may be that most minds are able to hear about them, read about them, or think about them, without feeling any promptings to commit a sinful act. Even this, however, has large and numerous exceptions. There are plenty of foolish, inexperienced and roughly-educated boys and girls to whom descriptions of violence, blood, drunkenness, and riot, are exciting in a dangerous degree. Pictures of crime, of impossible heroes and heroines, of romantic marriages and tragic adventures, excite that curiosity, that restlessness and that strange desire to imitate, which are found in all human beings before time and sad experience have sobered them. But in matters relating to modesty and purity, there is far more danger; because the passions are, as a rule, much more easily stirred up in these things than in others which are against the laws of God and our nature. The duty, therefore, of all who fear God and would save their immortal souls, is perfectly clear. You cannot read about, dwell upon, or entertain in your heart and thought, any scene, description, sentiment, or feeling, which it would be wrong to put into act, or which urges and leads to sinful act. All such reading and indulgence of the imagination is sinful, either because they set up sinful thinking, or because they lead to sinful acts, or for both reasons.

Although these are elementary principles of Christian morality, it is by no means superfluous to state them and dwell upon them. The idea that there is no harm in thoughts and desires is not unknown, even among Catholics. It is not always easy to persuade those who are accustomed to the freedom of modern manners that it is sinful to dwell on immodest thoughts, or that it is a duty to restrain impure feelings, and to reject imaginations which defile the heart. The nature of man is such, that thoughts and suggestions of this kind, and of other kinds, are sure to trouble us as long as we live. But we are bound to use reasonable means to resist them; and, above all, we are bound to avoid those occasions which give rise to them, and never to expose our weakness to any temptation which it is in our power to avoid.

The occasions of sinful imagination which come through reading may not be absolutely the most dangerous; but they are so common and so easily found that they have a special danger of their own. There are many different kinds of evil reading. First, there are books which are absolutely obscene and immoral. All decent people are on their guard against these. They are only fit to be put in the fire. Yet they are multiplying amongst us. There is no need to say that all parents and responsible persons should quietly and carefully keep them out of the way of the young. It is true, no doubt, that no precaution or vigilance will prevent any one, young or old, from getting such books if he wishes. As to this, we can only trust to a careful bringing up, to the confessional, and to the grace of God. But care and watchfulness will do something, and will, at any rate, save innocent youth from stumbling unawares upon things that may prove their ruin in soul and body.

Next, there are the books which are not absolutely and grossly immoral, but which are sensual, soft, and suggestive. Of these it may be said that no one, as a rule, reads them except for sensual reasons. They are not generally masterpieces; but they gratify a morbid interest, and stimulate feelings which are never very far from sin. All stories or novels in which the passion of love is strongly and warmly depicted, come under this class. Such books are unhealthy to the last degree. They prematurely arouse, and unduly excite, what the spiritual soul can with difficulty control even under the most favourable circumstances. They sap all wholesomeness and manliness of character, and lead to selfishness, peevishness, and laziness. Such books as these lie about everywhere, and are read by rich and poor. Idle ladies read them; but so do business men, clerks, servants, and working people who thus not only do harm to them selves directly, but, by squandering their time, expose themselves to loss, and are tempted to dishonesty and neglect of duty. Catholics ought clearly to under stand that because a book is openly sold, and read, and talked about, it is not therefore lawful to read. The rule of restraint, and the law of mortification, hold in this as in other things. It is far better to be behind our friends in our acquaintance with the talk of the hour, than to have our minds stained by doubtful reading. Innocence may be smiled at, but it is respected. Even if we have to endure ridicule, we shall be the happier for taking the side of God and of purity. Let us not be deluded by the talk which is now so common that the time has come for certain serious aspects of morality to be openly and plainly discussed. This is not the Christian rule or teaching. Such problems may and must be discussed, and as plainly as need be; but not by idle laymen, young women, or curious boys. Such topics require training, gravity, and circumspection. But the writers who are now setting the fashion of throwing them to the multitude care little, we may be sure, for the interests of truth or reformation, provided they can stir up unpleasant curiosity, and sell their books.

It may be said with truth that all idle reading is hurtful and bad. To read, for honest recreation, even silly books that are not otherwise objectionable, need not be condemned. But continuous idle reading of romantic, sentimental, or exciting narratives, spoils one's life and causes a general laziness and looseness in one s whole nature, unfitting the mind for exertion and the body for self-denial. The inordinate reading of newspapers should be avoided on similar grounds. There are all kinds of newspapers and cheap periodicals good, bad, and indifferent. Catholics must remember that they are not to take the tone of their moral feelings from newspapers, but from the teaching and traditions of their holy religion. It cannot be denied that there is, on the whole, a very free and lax interpretation, on the part of the newspaper press, of that precept of St. Paul which prescribes that certain things should "not be so much as named " among Christians (Ephesians v. 3). Because a matter is reported in a newspaper, it by no means follows that it is right or proper for a Christian to read it, much less to dwell upon it, or to let it get into the hands of those for whom one is responsible. The standard of right and wrong in things of this kind is constantly in danger of being lowered. Our duty is, by precept and by example, to uphold and maintain it. It may not be possible for us to do much in purifying the periodical press although the dis approval of God-fearing readers is never without its effect but we may at least preserve our own con science free from stain, and help many souls who otherwise would be carried away by the evil and corrupting tendencies of the age. Even when the newspaper is free from objection, it is easy to lose a great deal of time over it. It may be necessary or convenient to know what is going on in the world. But there can be no need of our absorbing all the rumours, all the guesses and gossip, all the petty incidents, all the innumerable paragraphs in which the solid news appears half drowned, like the houses and hedges when tbe floods are out. This is idle, and it is absolutely bad for brain and character. There is a kind of attraction towards petty and desultory reading of this kind which is sure to leave its mark on the present generation. The newspaper presents not only news, but ideas, reflections, views, inferences, and conclusions of every kind. As the reader takes in all this prepared and digested matter, he is deluded with the notion that he is thinking and exercising his mind. He is doing nothing of the kind. He is putting on another man s clothes, and fitting himself out with another man s ideas. To do this habitually is to live the life of a child; one is amused and occupied, and one is enabled to talk second-hand talk; but that is all. Men were better men, if they thought at all, in the days when there was less to read. It is pitiable to reflect how many there are, in all the ranks of life, who depend for ideas on the utterances of their newspapers. And who, after all, are the writers of newspapers? Men by no means specially endowed or qualified; men who have to write in a hurry, with little learning or training, on all kinds of subjects, some of them the most momentous; and men who have strong temptations to speak rashly and flippantly on all things connected with religion and morality. Immoderate newspaper reading leads, therefore, to much loss of time, and does no good, either to the mind or to the heart.

Books and periodicals which are calculated to weaken or pervert our religious faith are to be avoided, like immoral books. This is a duty which springs from the natural law, and is quite antecedent to any prohibition on the part of the Church. The Catholic should, therefore, refrain from reading anti-Catholic or anti-religious books. The arguments of such books may be, and probably have been, abundantly refuted. But the refutation is not always at hand, and it is not every reader who knows how to answer. There are in existence, unfortunately, at the present moment, many books of undoubted literary ability and interest which attack, generally in an in direct way, the existence of God, the divinity of our Lord, the Church, and man's moral responsibility. When the Catholic layman reads these productions, as he does far too freely, he is astonished and disturbed to find so strong a case made out against his faith. But why is he astonished and puzzled? It is generally because he knows so very little about his own religion. He has learnt his Catechism, perhaps, as a child, and has heard a sermon now and then; but the evidences, the explanations, and exposition of Christian doctrine have had little or no interest for him; and hence he is more or less at the mercy of the heretic and the sophist. It is evident that men and women of so little instruction have no right to expose themselves to the arguments of the enemy. And when they do come across such arguments, in their newspapers or general reading, they should know that it is chiefly their own ignorance that makes the difficulties seem so formidable. The

Church, if she had her own way, would keep such writings out of the hands of her children. No book which is known to be prohibited should be read by any Catholic, at least without proper advice.

If bad and indiscreet reading is productive of much harm, there is no limit to the possibilities of spiritual profit which arise from good reading. A good book is a faithful teacher, a true and faithful friend, and a never-failing helper in the things that concern salvation. Few Catholics take a proper view of the usefulness and the advantage of being well instructed in their religion. If a man s mind and heart are to take hold of his religion and to keep hold of it, his religion must be, by some means or other, worked into his mind and heart. The mind has many faculties, and so has the heart and imagination. Therefore, to grasp one's holy faith firmly and lovingly one must reason about it, one must follow it to conclusions and results, one must view it in the varying lights of history, of science, and of society, one must survey it as it touches the world at a thousand points, and feel it as it ministers to the innumerable aspirations of one s own nature. This kind of instruction is begun in childhood, when the teacher and the priest at the altar first bring the young intelligence of the child and its dawning sensibility face to face with God, with Christ, and with the sacraments. But by the time the young man or woman takes up the work of life it cannot be more than begun. How can it be continued and extended? The answer is, chiefly by reading. The spoken instructions of the Church s ministers are most profitable, and priests in charge of souls endeavour to obey the holy Council of Trent and to mingle instruction with all their exhortations. But a book will go further, and make things more secure. Since in these days all, or nearly all, are able to read, and to read easily, there ought undoubtedly to be a great advance on the part of Catholics in the knowledge of religion by means of print. And, happily, it cannot be pretended that there is nothing to read. If we consider, for example, the list of the publications of the Catholic Truth Society, we find among them instructions of every kind: exposition of doctrine, controversy, history, biography, devotion, and moral and social papers, besides tales and verse. No one is too poor to be able to afford the halfpenny or the penny which is the price of most of these brochures and leaflets; whilst there are books and larger pamphlets for those who look for something more extended, and the bound volumes of the series form a small library of the handiest and the most useful kind. For readers of greater education and leisure there are materials in abundance which it is unnecessary to specify at this moment. A catalogue of any of our London, Dublin, or New York Catholic publishers, will suggest to every one how many subjects there are on which it would be useful to be well-informed, and how much there is to be known in the grand and wide Kingdom of the holy Catholic faith. [42] No one can love Our Lord who does not know about Him, and no one can be truly loyal to the Church who does not take the trouble to study her.

If instruction is so deeply important, devotion and piety are not less so. With most of us, prayer is very short and very slight. There is one means which will both make us more regular in our daily prayer, and deepen our earnestness in that sacred duty. This is, Spiritual Reading. If our reading were merely instruction and information about God and divine things, our prayers would be all the better for it. To know more of the things of the Kingdom of Heaven is to walk abroad in the sunshine of a glorious universe whose very sight lifts us above the earth and inclines the heart to seek God. But when, in addition, we find in our book devout thoughts, pious aspirations, good advice, solid exhortation, and the example of the Saints, then the minutes of our prayer, which before seemed hard to fill up, overflow with the outpourings of a heart which all these things stimulate and inflame. No one should be without a book about Our Lord, His Sacred Heart, His blessed Mother, or the Saints. No one should be without a book on the Mass. Besides one's prayer-book, one should have manuals of meditation and of instruction on Christian virtues. More extended devotional treatises will keep alive the piety of those for whom they are suitable. But all Catholics, whatever their condition, should make use of Spiritual Reading. It is impossible to exaggerate the effect on the lives and characters of Christians of the words of holy men, of the heroic acts of the martyrs, of the example of the lovers of Jesus in every age, of the contemplation of Our Lady s prerogatives and goodness, and above all of the story of Our Lord and Saviour Jesus Christ.

The "Following of Christ," the "Spiritual Combat," the "Devout Life" of St. Francis de Sales, and other books of a like nature, are at once a guide to virtue, an encouragement to prayer, and an influence

---

[42]   Saint Pius X Press www.stpiusxpress.com has preserved over a thousand good Catholics books from tried and true authors prior to Vatican Ii.

drawing the heart daily nearer to God. The reading of Holy Scripture, of the sermons and conferences of distinguished preachers, and of the penetrating devotional books in which our language is by no means deficient, is adapted to sanctify the house, and to keep out of it, to a greater or less degree, that flood of objectionable printed matter which overflows the land at the present moment. Priests and laity cannot do more for souls than to encourage by every means in their power good and cheap Catholic literature instruction, devotion, tales, and periodicals and to bring it within the reach of every class of the faith ful. All read; they must read, and they will read. Let us strive to check the evils of bad reading by the dissemination of that which is good.

Bad Books

from <u>The Sinner's Return to God</u>, by Michael Muller

The foregoing chapter has been devoted to showing the necessity of avoiding the proximate occasion of sin. There is one special occasion of sin which must be dwelt upon more at length. It is the reading of bad books. Bad books are, 1, idle, useless books which do no good, but distract the mind from what is good; 2. Many novels and romances which do not appear to be so bad, but often are bad; 3. Books which treat professedly of bad subjects; 4. Bad newspapers, journals, miscellanies, sensational magazines, weeklies, illustrated papers, medical works; 5. Superstitious books, books of fate, etc.; 6. Protestant and infidel books and tracts.

There are certain idle, useless books which, though not bad in themselves, are pernicious because they cause the reader to lose the time which he might and ought to spend in occupations more beneficial to his soul. He who has spent much time in reading such books, and then goes to prayer, to Mass, and to Holy Communion, instead of thinking of God and of making acts of love and confidence, will be constantly troubled with distractions; for the representations of all the vanities he has read will be constantly present to his mind.

The mill grinds the corn which it receives. If the wheat be bad, how can the mill turn out good flour? How is it possible to think often of God, and offer to Him frequent acts of love, of oblation, of petition, and the like, if the mind is constantly filled with the trash read in idle, useless books? In his letter to his disciple Eustochium, St. Jerome stated for her instruction that in his solitude at Bethlehem he was attached to, and frequently read, the works of Cicero, and that he felt a certain disgust for pious books because their style was not polished. Almighty God, foreseeing the harm of this profane reading, and that without the aid of holy books the saint would never reach that height of sanctity for which he was destined, administered a remedy very harsh, no doubt, but well calculated to make him alive to his fault. He sent a grievous sickness on him, which soon brought the solitary to the brink of the grave. As he was lying at the point of death, God called him in spirit before His tribunal. The saint, being there, heard the Judge ask him who he was. He answered unhesitatingly, "I am a Christian; I hold no other faith than Thine, my Lord, my Judge." "Thou liest.," said the Judge; "thou art a Ciceronian, for where thy treasure is, there thy heart is also." He then ordered him to be severely scourged. The servant of God shrieked with pain as he felt the blows, and begged for mercy, repeating in a loud voice, "Have mercy upon me, O Lord! have mercy upon me." Meanwhile, they who stood round the throne of that angry Judge, falling on their faces before Him, began to plead in behalf of the culprit, implored mercy for him, and promised in his name that his fault should be corrected. Then St. Jerome, who, smarting with pain from the hard strokes he had received, would gladly have promised much greater things, began to promise and to swear, with all the ardor of his soul, that never again would he open profane; and worldly works, but that he would read pious, edifying books. As he uttered these words he returned to his senses, to the amazement of the bystanders, who had believed him to be already dead. St. Jerome concludes the narration of this sad history with these words: "Let no one fancy that it was an idle dream, like to those which come to deceive our minds in the dead of night. I call to witness the dread tribunal before which I lay prostrate, that it was no dream, but a true representation of a real occurrence; for when I returned to myself, found my eyes swimming with tears, and my shoulders livid and bruised with those cruel blows." He tells us, finally, that after this warning he devoted himself to the reading of pious books with the same diligence and zeal that he had before bestowed upon the works of profane writers. It was thus that Almighty God induced him to that study of divine things which was so essential to his own progress in perfection, and destined to do so much good to the whole Christian world.

It is true that in works like those of Cicero we sometimes find useful sentiments; but the same St. Jerome wisely said in a letter to another disciple: "What need have you of seeking for a little gold in the midst of so much dross, when you can read pious books in which yon shall find all gold without any dross?"

As to novels, they are, in general, pictures, and usually very highly wrought pictures, of human passions. Passion is represented as working out its ends successfully, and attaining its objects even by the sacrifice of duty. These books, as a class, present false views of life; and as it is the error of the young to mistake these for realities, they become the dupes of their own ardent and enthusiastic imaginations, which, instead of trying to control, they actually nourish with the poisonous food of phantoms and chimeras.

When the thirst for novel-reading has become insatiaable-as with indulgence it is sure to do-they come at last to live in an unreal fairy-land, amidst absurd heroes and heroines of their own creation, thus unfitting themselves for the discharge of the common duties of this every-day world, and for association with every-day mortals. The more strongly works of fiction appeal to the imagination, and the wider the field they afford for its exercise, the greater in general are their perilous attractions; and it is but too true that they cast, at last, a sort of spell over the mind, so completely fascinating the attention that duty is forgotten and positive obligation laid aside to gratify the desire of unravelling, to its last intricacy, the finely-spun web of some airy creation of fancy. Fictitious feelings are excited, unreal sympathies aroused, unmeaning sensibilities evoked. The mind is weakened; it has lost that laudable thirst after truth which God has imprinted on it; filled with a baneful love of trifles, vanity, and folly, it has no taste for serious reading and profitable occupations; all relish for prayer, for the Word of God, for the reception of the sacraments, is lost; and, at last, conscience and common sense give place to the dominion of unchecked imagination. Such reading, instead of forming the heart, depraves it. It poisons the morals and excites the passions; it changes all the good inclinations a person has received from nature and a virtuous education; it chills by little and little pious desires, and in a short time banishes out of the soul all that was there of solidity and virtue. By such reading, young girls on a sudden lose a habit of reservedness and modesty, take an air of vanity and frivolity, and make show of no other ardor than for those things which the world esteems and which God abominates. They espouse the maxims, spirit, conduct, and language of the passions which are there under various disguises artfully instilled into their minds; and, what is most dangerous, they cloak all this irregularity with the appearances of civility and an easy, complying, gay humor and disposition.

St. Teresa, who fell into this dangerous snare of reading idle books, writes thus of herself: "This fault failed not to cool my good desires, and was the cause of my falling insensibly into other defects. I was so enchanted with the extreme pleasure I took herein that I thought I could not be content if I had not some new romance in my hands. I began to imitate the mode, to take delight in being well dressed, to take great care of my hands, to make use of perfumes, and to affect all the vain trimmings which my condition admitted. Indeed, my intention was not bad, for I would not for the world, in the immoderate passion which I had to be decent, give anyone an occasion of offending God; but I now acknowledge how far these things, which for several years appeared to me innocent, are effectually and really criminal."

Criminal and dangerous, therefore, is the disposition of those who fritter away their time in reading such books as fill the mind with a worldly spirit, with a love of vanity, pleasure, idleness, and trifling; which destroy and lay waste all the generous sentiments of virtue in the heart, and sow there the seeds of every vice. Who seeks nourishment from poisons? Our thoughts and reflection are to the mind what food is to the body; for by them the affections of the soul are nourished. The chameleon changes its color as it is affected by pain, anger, or pleasure, or by the color upon which it sits; and we see an insect borrow its lustre and hue from the plant or leaf upon which it feeds. In like manner, what our meditations and affections are, such will our souls become-either holy and spiritual or earthly and carnal.

In addition to their other dangers, many of these books unfortunately teem with maxims subversive of faith in the truths of religion. The current popular literature in our day is penetrated with the spirit of licentiousness, from the pretentious quarterly to the arrogant and flippant daily newspaper, and the weekly and monthly publications are mostly heathen or maudlin. They express and inculcate, on the one hand, stoical, cold, and polished pride of mere intellect, or, on the other, empty and wretched sentimentality. Some employ the skill of the engraver to caricature the institutions and offices of the Christian religion, and others to exhibit the grossest forms of vice and the most distressing scenes of crime and suffering. The illustrated press has become to us what the amphitheatre was to the Romans when men were slain, women were outraged, and Christians given to the lions to please a degenerate populace. "The slime of the serpent is over it all." It instills the deadly poison of irreligion and immorality through every pore of the reader. The fatal miasma floats in the whole literary atmosphere, is drawn ill with every literary breath, corrupting the very life-blood of religion in the mind and soul. Thus it frequently happens that the habitual perusal of such books soon banishes faith from the soul, and in its stead introduces infidelity. He who often reads bad books will soon be filled with the spirit of the author who wrote them. The first author of pious books is the Spirit of God; but the author of bad books is the devil, who artfully conceals from certain persons the poison which such works contain. Written, as they generally are in a most attractive, flowery style, the reader becomes enchanted, as it were, by their perusal, not suspecting the poison that lies hidden under that beautiful style, and which he drinks as he reads on.

But it is objected the book is not so bad. Of what do bad books treat? What religion do they teach? Many of them teach either deism, atheism, or pantheism? Others ridicule our holy religion and everything that is sacred. What morals do these books teach? The most lewd. Vice and crime are deified; monsters of humanity are held out as true heroes. Some of these books speak openly and shamelessly of the most obscene things, whilst others do so secretly, hiding their poison under a flowery style. They are only the more dangerous because their poisonous contents enter the heart unawares.

A person was very sorry to see that a certain bad book was doing so much harm. He thought he would read it, that he might be better able to speak against it. With this object in view he read the book. The end of it was that instead of helping others he ruined himself.

Some say, "I read bad books on account of the style. I wish to improve my own style. I wish to learn something of the world." This is no sufficient reason for reading such books. The good style of a book does not make its poisonous contents harmless. A fine dress may cover a deformed body, but it cannot take away its deformity. Poisonous serpents and flowers may be very beautiful, but for all that they are not the less poisonous. To say that such books are read purely because of their style is not true, because those who allege this as an excuse sometimes read novels which are written in a bad style. There are plenty of good books, written in excellent style, which are sadly neglected by these lovers of pure English.

To consult those books for a knowledge of the world is another common excuse for their perusal. Well, where shall we find an example of one who became a deeper thinker, a more eloquent speaker, a more expert business man, by reading novels and bad books? They only teach how to sin, as Satan taught Adam and Eve to eat of the forbidden tree, under the pretence of attaining real knowledge; and the result was loss of innocence, peace, and Paradise, and the punishment of the human race through all time.

Some profess to skip the bad portions and read only the good. But how are they to know which are the bad portions unless they read them? The pretext is a false one. He only will leave the bad who hates it. But he who hates the bad things will not read the books at all, unless he be obliged to do so; and no one is obliged to read them, for there are plenty of good, profitable, and entertaining books which can be read without danger.

There is a class of readers who flatter themselves that bad books may hurt others, but not them; they make no impression on them. Happy and superior mortals! Are they gifted with hearts of stone, or of flesh and blood? Have they no passions? Why should these books hurt others and not them? Is it because they are more virtuous than others? Is it not true that the bad, obscene parts of. the story remain more vividly and deeply impressed upon their minds than those which are more or less harmless? Did not the perusal of these books sometimes cause those imaginations and desires forbidden by Christian modesty? Did they not sometimes accuse themselves in confession of having read them? If not, they ought to have done so. Who would like to die with such a book in their hand? Readers of bad books who say such reading does not affect them should examine themselves and see whether they are not blinded by their passions, or so far gone in crime that, like an addled egg, they cannot become more corrupt than they already are.

See that infamous young man, that corrupter of innocence. What is the first step often of a young reprobate who wishes to corrupt some poor, innocent girl? He first lends her a bad book. He believes that if she reads that book she is lost. A bad book, as he knows, is an agreeable corrupter; for it veils vice under a veil of flowers. It is a shameless corrupter. The most licentious would blush, would hesitate to speak the language that their eyes feed on. But a bad book does not blush, feels no shame, no hesitation. Itself unmoved and silent, it places before the heart and imagination the most shameful obscenities.

A bad book is a corrupter to whom the reader listens without shame, because it can be read alone and taken up when one pleases.

Go to the hospitals and brothels; ask that young man who is dying of a shameful disease; ask that young woman who has lost her honor and her happiness; go to the dark grave of the suicide; ask them what was the first step in their downward career, and they will answer, the reading of bad books.

Not long ago a young lady from Poughkeepsie, N. Y., who was once a good Catholic, began to read novels. Not long after she wished to imitate what she read, and to become a great lady. So she left her comfortable home, and ran away with another young lady to New York. There she changed her name, became a drunkard and a harlot, and even went so far in her wickedness as to kill a policeman. Here is the story, told in the woman's own words as given in the public press:

Fanny Wright, the woman who killed police officer McChesney, in New York, on the night of November 2, has been removed to the Tombs, and now occupies a cell in the upper tier of the female prison. The clothing stained with blood of her victim, which she has worn since her arrest, has been changed. In reply to interrogations she made the following statements respecting her life:

"About ten years ago I was living happily with my parents at Poughkeepsie, in this State. Nothing that I wished for was withheld. I was trained in the Roman Catholic faith, and attended to my religions duties with carefulness and pleasure until I was corrupted by a young girl of the same age, who was my school-fellow. She had been reading novels to such an extent that her head had become fairly upset, and nothing would do her but to travel and see the world. The dull life of a small country place like Poughkeepsie would not suit her tastes and inclinations, and from repeatedly whispering into my ears and persuading me that we would be great ladies, have horses, carriages, diamonds, and servants of our own, I finally reluctantly consented to flee from home, and we started together one beautiful night for the city of New York. [Here the poor woman gave way to tears, and sobbed hysterically.] On our arrival in this city we took up our quarters with Mrs. Adams, at No. 87 Leonard Street, and this was the place where I lost my virtue and commenced to lead a life of bitter, bitter shame. My family ultimately succeeded in finding out my whereabouts and took me home, but I could not listen to the voice of reason. I felt that I had selected my mode of life, and was determined at all hazards to follow it out. I escaped a second time, and went back to Mrs. Adams's, where I was confined of a sweet little girl shortly afterwards. I used to keep myself very clean, and dressed with great care and tastefulness. From Mrs. Adams's I moved to Mrs. Willoughby's, at No. 101 Mercer Street, and lived there until the death of my little girl, three years ago; that had an awful effect upon me; I could not help taking to drink to drown my sorrow. From this period I date the commencement of my real hardships. My father emigrated to California, and I had no one left but a young brother; he tried to reform me, and also his poor wife; God bless her! she used to cry herself sick at my disgrace. Previous to this the young girl who accompanied me from home in the first instance fell out lucky, and got married. Drinking was the only pleasure of my life, and it was not long until it began to have its results; I was arrested and committed to the Island for six months; I got down before my time was up, and again took to liquor and street-walking. I used to walk all the time between Greene, Wooster, and Mercer Streets, in the Eighth Ward. I was soon arrested the second time, and sent up again for six months. During the last three years of my life, I have been sent on the Island six times altogether for drunkenness and disorderly conduct. On the night the officer was killed [here she gave way again to tears, and rocked herself around on the bed in a fearful manner], I was walking through the street, going home with a message, and picking the kernels out of a hickory-nut with a small knife, when the officer came up to me; I was almost drunk at the time, and much excited; I did not know what I was doing, when on the impulse of the moment I struck him with the knife and I killed him." On Tuesday the brother of Fanny, a respectable young man, residing in the neighborhood of Poughkeepsie, called at the prison and had an interview with his sister.

A more affecting scene, says the Express it has seldom been our lot to witness. Although a strong, robust man, he fairly shook with emotion from his keen sense of grief and shame. He remained with her for nearly an hour. She was almost frantic with violent outbursts of grief, and after his departure became insensible.

Another young lady of the State of New York was sent to a convent school, where she received a brilliant education. She spoke seven languages. She wished to enter a convent, but was prevented by her parents. Her parents died, and after their death the young lady took to novel-reading. She soon wished to imitate what she had read; she wished to become a heroine. So she went upon the stage and danced in the "Black Crook." At last she fell one day on Second Avenue, in New York, and broke her leg in six places. She was taken to a hospital, where a good lady gave her a prayer-book. But she flung it away and asked for a novel. She would not listen to the priest encouraging her to make her confession and be reconciled to God. She died impenitent, with a novel in her hand.

Assuredly, if we are bound by every principle of our religion to avoid bad company, we are equally bound to avoid bad books; for of all evil, corrupting company, the worst is a bad book. There can be no doubt that the most pernicious influences at work in the world at this moment come from bad books and bad newspapers. The yellow-covered literature, as it is called, is a pestilence compared with which the yellow fever, and cholera, and small-pox are as nothing, and yet there is no quarantine against it. Never take a book into your hands which you would not be seen reading. Avoid not only notoriously immoral books and papers, but avoid also all those miserable sensational magazines and novels and illustrated papers which are so profusely scattered around on every side. The demand which exists for such garbage speaks badly for the moral sense and intellectual training of those who read them. If you wish to keep your mind pure and your soul in the grace of God, you must make it so firm and steady principle of conduct never to touch them.

Would you be willing to pay a man for poisoning your food? And why should you be fool enough to pay the authors and publishers of bad books and pamphlets, magazincs, and the editors of irreligious newspapers for poisoning your soul with their impious principles and their shameful stories and pictures?

Go, then, and burn all bad books in your possession, even if they do not belong to you, even if they are costly. Two boys in New York bought a bad picture with their pocket-money, and burned it. A young man in Augusta, Ga., spent twenty dollars in buying up bad books and papers to burn them all. A modern traveller tells us that when he came to Evora, he there on Sunday morning conversed with a girl in the kitchen of the inn. He examined some of her books which she showed him, and told her that one of them was written by an infidel, whose sole aim was to bring all religion into contempt. She made no reply to this, but, going into another room, returned with her apron full of dry sticks, all of which she piled upon the fire and produced a blaze. She then took that bad book and placed it upon the flaming pile; then, sitting down, she took her rosary out of her pocket, and told her beads until the book was entirely burnt up.

In the Acts of the Apostles we read that when St. Paul preached at Ephesus, many of the Jews and Gentiles were converted to the faith. "And many of them that believed came confessing and declaring their deeds. And many of those who had followed curious arts brought together their books and burnt them before all. And counting the price of them, they found the money to be fifty thousand pieces of silver."

A young nobleman who was on a sea voyage began to read an obscene book in which he took much pleasure. A religious priest, on noticing it, said to him: "Are you disposed to make a present to Our Blessed Lady?" The young man replied that he was. "Well," said the priest, "I wish that, for the love of the most holy Virgin, you would give up that book and throw it into the sea." "Here it is, father," answered the young man. "No," replied the priest, "you must yourself make this present to Mary." He did so at once. Mary was not slow in rewarding the nobleman for the great promptness with which he cast the bad book into the sea; for no sooner had he returned to Genoa, his native place, than the Mother of God so inflamed his heart with divine love that he entered a religious order.

115

Bad Reading

From <u>Theory and Practice of the Confessional</u>

The reading of bad books is a source of great danger, and this occasion of sin is very common, unceasingly estranging countless numbers from faith and robbing them of innocence.

We must distinguish between: (1) books which, ex professo, (avowedly) are written against religion and faith (defending the errors of heretics and infidels) and those which are not, ex professo, directed against it (only here and there attacking religion); (2) books which, ex professo, are obscene (which, if not wholly, yet to a great extent, treat of obscene things) and such as are subobscoeni (in which a good deal of obscenity is to be found) .

Books ex professo impii (avowedly impious) are very dangerous and pernicious.

Few persons who are not learned and pious theologians can read them without injury to their faith. Hence the Church (in the second rule of the Index) has strictly prohibited the reading of such books, and if they haeresim propugnant, (promote heresy) reading them consciously entails censure of excommunication reserved to the Pope. [43] Books which are hostile to religion, but not so ex professo, are also a source of danger, and, therefore, reading them is permitted to no one without necessity. The degree of the danger depends upon the object which the reader has in view, upon his age, his religious sentiments, and knowledge.

Books ex professo obscene are certainly dangerous, for they excite violent temptations, and they are still worse when, as is often the case, they are illustrated with obscene pictures. Reading such is strictly forbidden by the seventh rule of the Index.

The libri erotici (de amoribus agentes), (erotic books) for instance many comedies, tragedies, dramas, novels, and romances, are sources of relative danger; the reading of them is, in many respects, injurious, especially to young people.

---

[43] Compare 43; S. Alph. App. de prohib. libr. cp. 1; cf . Benger, Pastoraltheologie (2 Ed.), Vol. II. 129, n. 7, p. 53 ff .; Clement XIII, Encycl. 1766; Pius IX, Qui Pluribus," 20 Nov., 1846 j many pastorals of bishops.

Bad newspapers and periodicals must be classified in the same way as books, and what has been said above concerning the reading of bad books holds good as to newspapers and periodicals. If they are written ex professo against faith and morals, they are even more dangerous than such books.

Accordingly, the confessor is bound: (1) when there is ground for suspicion that the penitent has sinned by such reading and has been silent about it, to ask him on the matter; omitting to do so would be very injurious to the penitent, as it would be leaving him in great danger, and if he had purposely concealed it, he would have confessed sacrilegiously.

The confessor is bound (2) to admonish penitents who have read bad books, etc., to refrain entirely from such reading, to buy no more books, etc., of the kind, not to borrow them, nor in future to have them in their possession. He must especially instruct parents and superiors on this head, and incite them to watchfulness. He is bound (3) to refuse absolution to those who will not refrain from such reading. [44] (4) To prescribe for the penitent who reads infidel writings ex necessitate suitable safe guards in order that the poison may not injure him, such remedies as reading good books and newspapers, praying for the preservation of faith, frequent reception of the Sacraments, etc. (5) To do his best to keep young people from novel reading. [45]

The confessor must, to the best of his ability, endeavor to prevent the reading of so-called "liberal" books, newspapers, and periodicals, which are, indeed, bad, though not, ex professo, godless or obscene; especially (a) when the penitent is conscious of his duty to refrain from such reading, or is in doubt about it; (b) when, although not aware of this duty, good results are to be expected from exhortation; and (c) when the confessor perceives that such reading is beginning to harm the penitent. On the other hand, the confessor must be silent concerning the duty of avoiding such reading (a) when the penitent is invincibiliter (invincibly) [46] ignorant of this duty; (6) when the confessor could not hope that his admonition would be acted upon,

---

[44]Cf. Propos. 61 damn, ab Innoc. XI. The condemned proposition is: "He can sometimes be absolved, who remains in a proximate occasion of sinning, which he can and does not wish to omit, but rather directly and professedly seeks or enters into."

[45]Cf. S. Alph. Lib. III. n. 429.

[46]Invincible ignorance should be overcome by studying the truth.

or when, on the contrary, he would have to fear still greater evils; but he must then inspire his penitent with distrust of these newspapers, etc., and endeavor by exhortation and request to wean him from such dangerous reading. [47] A man of business might be permitted to keep and to read bad newspapers on account of the advertisements, when such advertisements are not to be found (or not so fully) in a good paper, but he must be admonished to subscribe for this end only, and not to leave the newspaper about for others, especially children, to read. It is not allowed to inn-keepers to have bad newspapers in their establishments in order to attract customers by such reading, for that would be an actio ex se ordinata ad malum. (an action of itself evil.) Under the heading of "bad newspapers" are not included those producing here and there incorrect judgments upon religion. [48]

The Reading of Bad Books

From <u>Sermon Matter</u> by Fr. Ferreol Girardey

1. We often hear these and similar assertions: "We live in an enlightened age. The human mind is progressive and should be emancipated from all ancient, obsolete, undue restrictions, for it is now fully able to judge for itself. Liberty of thought, liberty of speech, liberty of the press, is the offspring of modern civilisation. I read both sides, the pro and the con, so that I may not remain behind the age, but may keep up with the times, with modern progress. I am free to read what I like. I am old enough to know what is good and what is bad for me. I am well qualified to judge for myself. I am my own master; it is nobody's business what I read. I need relaxation; I can not always work or pray." Well, how much do you pray?

"I read out of curiosity, to be up-to-date in everything." But why read such stuff?

"I read to acquire a knowledge of mankind,." But fiction, being fiction and not reality, can give you only a fictitious knowledge of men.

---

[47] Cf. Aertnys, 1. c. n. 331, Q. II.
[48] Cf. Aertnys, 1. c. n. 330, Q. II; Gury, Tom. T. n. 256; Varceno, Theol. Mor. Tract. 8, cp. 2, art. 3; Berardi, Praxis Conf . nn. G6 et 240; M tiller, Theol. Mor. Lib. II. 36, n. 6.

"I read those books on account of their fine style." You are like a man who likes a good cake and, seeing a number of fine cakes immersed in the mire, picks them up and eats them!

"I read those books to acquire a fine style." What profit has your style derived from such filthy and erroneous matter? I suppose you thought more of gratifying your morbid curiosity in reading such trash than of analyzing its style and trying to conform yours to it. And even if you derived any profit therefrom for your style, it was at too great an expense, for it cost you your lively faith, your innocence, your virtue; irreparable expenses for you.

"Religious and pious books are dry and poorly written." Where did you find that out? Surely not from reading many of them.

"I read those books to drive away the blues, to drown my troubles." And with what success? Tell me candidly, whether it would not be better and more consoling and satis factory for you to say a few prayers, to visit our divine Saviour in the Sacrament of His love, to bear your troubles for the love of Jesus crucified. Try it and you will be astonished at the good results.

"I know my religion; the books I read can do me no harm." We shall now see that you are mistaken.

2. Bad books, bad pamphlets, bad papers are one of the greatest scourges of religion, of morality, of society itself. Reading is food for the mind. Our mind or reason is the guide of our will, of our conduct. Bad reading of every kind poisons the mind. "The just man liveth by faith " (Rom. I. 17). But bad books destroy the reader's faith, either directly or indirectly; directly, if they treat of theo logical or philosophical subjects, for they fill the mind with false principles; indirectly, if they sap true morality, like a large number of novels, because they corrupt the reader's morals, and corruption of morals destroys first the reader's practical faith and gradually his theoretical faith, that is his belief in the doctrines of faith. Let us bear in mind that in this life we have nothing greater, nothing more precious than the gift of faith, for "without faith it is impossible to please God" (Hebr. n. 6), and save our soul (Mark 16. 16). Bad books are the scourge of morality, for religion is the basis of morality; there is no such a thing as morality without God honored as supreme Lawgiver, and therefore no morality without religion, for it alone teaches us to give due honor to God. Bad books are the scourge of society, for the basis of human

society is necessarily morality and religion, as even the pagans of old admitted. Therefore bad books, by undermining religion, undermine all morality and the welfare and permanence of society. Bad books are the scourge of the family. The family is the result of marriage, which should necessarily be holy and indissoluble. The children owe their parents respect, obedience and love. But what do bad books teach? They teach that marriage is a mere contract, and therefore dissoluble; that it is not holy, but only a means of gratifying the passions, of promoting temporal interests; they deal in adultery which they call gallantry, praise divorce as a progress of civilisation, free love as a want of nature; they decry virtue and piety as chimeras, as hypocrisy, bigotry, and modesty and purity as a weakness, as contrary to nature; and ridicule the parents who require subordination and moral behavior from their children.

3. The usual effects of the passionate reading of works of fiction, on account of their sentimental style, their pictures of profane, passionate love, of the love of the sensual man, their making the gratification of the passions the highest possible enjoyment. All this tends to crush out heroic virtue, all true manliness, and leads, first, to loss of innocence and corruption of heart; the heart once corrupt the reader soon becomes disgusted with all serious reading, such as history, religious books; then follows gradual loss of faith, disinclination to honest labor, to the practice of the domestic virtues, a sort of frenzy for pleasure and romantic adventures, indifference to reputation, loss of bodily and mental health, and finally disgust for everything and even for life; and for many the end is suicide! [49]

4. Tell me what you read, and I will tell you what you think, what you believe, and what you feel, for bad reading ruins both the soul and the body. The eye reads, the memory retains, the imagination represents, the sensuality is excited, the reason is led astray, and the will follows the reason. Hence, in the first place, the loss of faith results from reading books that misrepresent the Catholic faith, its doctrines and practices and the clergy. Secondly, the passionate reading of novels and the like results, as we have just seen, in the loss of purity and modesty and in its consequences. Bad reading does not at once end in the loss of faith and innocence; nor does it usually at first make a bad

---

[49]   Look at the state of *morality* today. One readily sees that all of this has happened and more.

impression on the reader, but awakens his curiosity and urges him on to continue the reading. It is like the battering-ram of the ancient Romans. By means of repeated blows of this engine of war against the thickest and strongest walls of a city, the walls would be battered down in the course of time, and thus the Roman army could enter through the breach and capture the city. In like manner, by repeatedly reading bad and dangerous books the virtue and faith of the reader will soon be battered down and unbelief and vice will find an unobstructed entrance into the mind and heart of the reader. Thirdly, experience proves that the passionate reading of works of fiction is injurious to the nervous system of the young, induces insomnia, and renders them unfit for domestic life, and not unfrequently leads to sinful habits, to insanity, and even to suicide.

5. The habit of novel reading by instilling into the mind fictitious ideas of real life, of the family, leads in contracting marriage to disobey the laws of the Church and even the laws of sound, common sense, for fiction deprives marriage of its very object, of its dignity, and banishes all really good motives for contracting it; therefore, such readers usually contract unhappy marriages, and, when married, do not rear their children, so as to secure either their temporal or eternal welfare!

6. The reading of bad books is very injurious to the Church. Such books declaim against and ridicule virginity, modesty, piety, self-denial, penance, humility and other virtues and laud pride, ambition, dangerous and sinful pleasures, the gratification of sensuality. They teach that it matters not what one believes, provided he is honest, that it is unmanly to submit one's reason to the teachings of the Church, and that every one is free to judge for himself in all matters whatever. In a word, such books so abound in false principles, that their readers are gradually led into unbelief and even into hatred of the Church and her teaching.

7. Bad books are most hurtful to the state. By their false teaching concerning marriage they undermine the family, and do great injury to the state for the family is the basis of society, since society, or the state, is composed of families and is perpetuated only by its families. They teach not only the lawfulness of divorce, but go so far as to make it appear advisable and even necessary, and thus aim at the destruction of society. Moreover, they advocate and spread the false

principles of secret societies, which are subversive of all order and authority, and are filled with the praises of men whose lives were filled with immoral and scandalous practices.

8. Bad books are hurtful to all readers. Three things are required to produce a bad effect: 1, a thing that is bad or injurious in itself; 2, a thing that is liable to be injured; 3, the union of both together. The principles taught by the authors of bad books undermine the faith; their descriptions have an immoral tendency, and their style is usually fascinating, blinding and seductive. The reader's faith lacks firmness, his virtue is inconstant and easily ruined, and he is easily impressed, enticed and led away by descriptions of things or events that appeal to his passions. Hence such readers will be carried away by the reading of bad books either to infidelity or immorality, or rather to the loss of both their innocence and their faith. Those whose faith and virtue are firm and constant, never read bad books, for they abhor them. The readers of bad books are not angels, but have strong and unsubdued passions; they are not well grounded in their faith, for they have only a confused idea of what it teaches; hence they are both morally and mentally unfit to withstand the bad effects of such reading.

9. CURE FOR BAD READING. In the first place, you must put away, or rather destroy such books, as the Christians at Ephesus did in the time of St. Paul : "Many of them who had followed curious arts, brought together their books, and burnt them before all; and counting the price of them, they found the money to be fifty thousand pieces of silver" (Acts 19. 19). How dare you keep what you should not read, and give occasion to others to read such books! You have no right to give away, to sell, to lend, to borrow or praise such books! This obliges you under pain of mortal sin! A pagan author, Valerius Maximus, says of a certain pagan nation: "They would not suffer the minds of their children to be imbued with such books, lest they should do greater harm to their morals than afford benefit to their minds." The infidel Diderot, the writer of so many bad books, seeing one day his daughter reading one of his own books, snatched it out of her hands and cast it into the fire, for, although he wrote books to corrupt the faith and morals of others, he did not wish to have his own daughter's faith and morals corrupted! He also took great care of her religious education and was accustomed to teach her the catechism regularly. The great infidel, Jean Jacques Rousseau, who by his writings ruined the faith and

morals of his cotemporaries and prepared the way for the French Revolution, was corrupted at the age of seven years by reading the novels left by his late deceased mother! On the other hand, what wonderful conversions have been wrought through the reading of good books! St. Augustine, who was converted by reading the life of St. Paul, the first hermit, mentions two courtiers of the Roman emperor who were converted by reading the life of the Abbot St. Antony of Egypt. St. Columban was converted by reading the life of St. Mary of Egypt, the penitent; and St. Ignatius by reading the Lives of the Saints. Good books instruct the ignorant, admonish the slothful, stir up the indifferent, stimulate the careless, correct the erring, and raise up the fallen! You should have in your homes a number of good Catholic books, and read them at least on Sundays. You should support the Catholic press by subscribing to some Catholic Magazine and to at least one Catholic paper. "The best and most intelligent Catholics," says the New Mission Book, "are usually those who read good Catholic books and papers. They take an interest in their faith; they know and appreciate it; they are also able to explain and defend it and they are always to be relied on when there is question of making sacrifices to maintain and spread their holy faith."

Additional Thoughts on the Same Subject

First of all we should read from a good spiritual book every day for a half an hour. Limiting this to Sundays is certainly not sufficient in these days of the Great Apostasy.

1. No one would like to taste poison to see how it tastes. In like manner, no one should read a bad book out of mere curiosity about its contents.

2. St. Bernard says : "Vain reading begets vain thoughts." Bad reading, therefore, begets evil thoughts.

3. St. Augustine says : "By bad reading we do not acquire eloquence nor a fine style, but become vicious thereby, and learn to know evil without abhorring it, to speak of it without shame, to commit it without restraint."

4. St. Jerome says : "Is it necessary for thee to plunge into the mire to pick up a bit of gold ore, when thou canst get a quantity of it elsewhere?"

5. St. Thomas says: "The reading of profane books, so pleasant to worldlings, corrupts the morals of the young, leads men to worldliness, sensual love and vice."

6. The Board of health makes strict regulations to prevent the spread of contagious diseases; in like manner, it is the duty of the Church to prevent the spreading of unbelief and vice among her children.

7. A fine style in a bad book is like a magnificent dress worn by a harlot.

8. Would you drink a delicious and sweet beverage mingled with a deadly poison?

9. No sane man would seek a healthy plant in a field of poisonous weeds.

10. "It is God who speaks to us, when we read a good book," says St. Jerome.

11. "Vain reading," says St. Bonaventure, "begets vain thoughts, and extinguishes devotion."

Conclusion

Saint Ambrose writes: "I am of the opinion that one should not only avoid frequent plays, but all plays." [50] A strong argument has just been made in favor of the total elimination of television in the lives of Catholics. That Catholics must live differently from the rest of the world is without question.

Saint Paul says:

"I beseech you therefore, brethren, by the mercy of God, that you present your bodies a, living sacrifice, holy, pleasing unto God your reasonable service. And be not conformed to this world: but be reformed in the newness of your mind, that you may prove what is the good and the acceptable and the perfect will of God." [51]

The world praises television and endeavors to get televisions in the hands of all. The world thinks that only a freak or a crazy person does not have a television. Saint Paul tells us that we must be fools for Christ. We must go contrary to what is politically correct and socially acceptable.

TEOTWAWKI

Soon we will experience The End Of The World As We Know It, the Three Days of Darkness. Soon we will all give up television. Just as movies, radio and television prepared the world for the Great Apostasy, in the chastisement God will soon send upon this sinful world all three will be taken away. Above we considered briefly the coming Three Days of Darkness. There is not space here to consider this in any detail. It is recommended to read The Coming Chastisement, which goes into far more detail. [52] One aspect of the Three Days of Darkness is the death of three quarters of the world population. With the death of this many people, the remaining people will be unable to keep the current system running. Electricity will cease to function. In fact, during the Three

---

[50]   Dignity and Duties of the Priest, Saint Alphonsus, page 351.
[51]   Romans 12:1-2
[52]   This can be obtained from the Vatican in Exile or on Amazon.

Days itself there apparently will be no electricity, because only blessed candles will give light. This may indicate that a solar flare will take down the electric grid about time the Chastisement begins.

Apocalypse warns:

> And I heard another voice from heaven, saying: Go out from her, my people; that you be not partakers of her sins and that you receive not of her plagues. For her sins have reached unto heaven: and the Lord hath remembered her iniquities. [53]

We can conclude from what has been presented that the average television viewer sins mortally several times a day in the perverse programs they watch and their participation in the sins of others. It is time for Catholics to step away from the world and its sins and prepare their souls for the Chastisement that will soon come upon the earth. It is time for Catholics to adhere to the unchanging rules of morality, rather to the lax teachings of the 20th and 21st centuries. The Fathers of the Church could have condemned television as would the countless saints over the centuries. We must join them in their condemnation and adhere to the strict rules they laid down for Christian living. True times have changed, but we cannot change with them. Time have changed for the worse not for the better. Sins that were socially unacceptable ten years ago are acceptable now. And we can thank the television in part for this sorry state of affairs.

More Information

It is suggested that people look into these matters seriously. Several books on the evils of television have been written over the last half of a century. Although they cannot be recommended without some reservations, because they are written by neo-pagans, they do have some good research.

Also the current condition of the Catholic Church must be understood completely, lest one find themselves in an heretical sect following the *doctrines of devils*. We have written <u>54 Years that Changed the Catholic Church</u> in order to address this in a simple manner.

---

[53]   Apocalypse 18:4-5

Those wishing to understand the coming chastisement are advised to read <u>The Coming Chastisement</u>.

All of our books are available on Amazon and through major book retailers, such as Barnes and Noble and Hastings.

Made in the USA
Middletown, DE
11 October 2020